"*The Lost World of the Flood* lays befo
of the text itself, an honesty about hyperbole in the flood narrative, a splendid locating
and explaining of the flood story in the context of the ancient Near East, a profound
grasp of the theological value of the text, and a noble example of how to read the Bible
as the Word of God. A brave and sound accomplishment."

Scot McKnight, Julius R. Mantey Chair of New Testament, Northern Seminary

"A 'plain sense' reading of the biblical flood account has been under siege since the inception of 'flood geology' nearly a century ago. In an effort to uphold the truth of Scripture, many well-intentioned Christians have instead ravaged both the biblical text and the field of geology. In *The Lost World of the Flood*, Longman and Walton make great strides in retrieving biblical authority from interpretations of Genesis 6 through 9 founded on poor exegesis and equally poor science. With a firm but gentle hand the authors lead their readers into the world of ancient Israel, offering an interpretation of the biblical flood narrative that honors the authority of Scripture and respects the scientific consensus on geological matters."

Kyle Greenwood, associate professor of Old Testament and Hebrew, Colorado Christian University

"Two scholars of the ancient Near East and the Bible join a geologist to address a vexing question from Genesis: What was the nature and extent of the biblical flood? With clarity and logic, they present a position counter to traditional evangelical 'orthodoxy' but which, if seeking to be rebutted, will need to be addressed with equal clarity and logic."

David W. Baker, professor of Old Testament and Semitic languages, Ashland Theological Seminary

"In *The Lost World of the Flood,* John Walton and Tremper Longman III continue Walton's earlier work in his Lost World series, in this case connecting the flood and Babel narratives of Genesis chapters 6–11 to the earlier chapters, Abraham, and even events and sermons recorded in the New Testament. Walton and Longman examine the Mesopotamian geographic and cultural context for the pre-Abrahamic Genesis narrative. They demonstrate that the deliberate employment of selected historical vignettes in the early chapters of Genesis is rhetorically shaped. Significantly, Walton and Longman establish the role that hyperbolic language plays in the Genesis appropriation of its cultural backdrop. By so doing, they explain why the flood of Noah must refer to a significant regional event, not a planetary-scale cataclysm. They press a strong claim that those who attempt to ignore the original revelatory clientele are arrogating authority to themselves. If they are correct, then many assertions by those proposing a global tsunami-like flood are overconfident at best and misleading at worst. Walton and Longman deserve a lot of praise for their insightful approach and therapeutic discussion of the Noah narrative."

Ralph Stearley, professor of geography and environmental studies, Calvin College

"The authors have provided yet another excellent Lost World volume for readers who seek a deep dive into this controversial topic in order to strengthen their faith. This volume will be a great help to all who exemplify faith seeking understanding."

Bill T. Arnold, Paul S. Amos Professor of Old Testament Interpretation, Asbury Theological Seminary

"John Walton, the Indiana Jones of biblical Lost Worlds, has done it again! After maneuvering through the thickets and surveying the topography of the ancient Near Eastern cultural landscape of the Lost Worlds of Genesis 1, Scripture, and Adam and Eve, Walton maps the terrain of the Lost World of the Flood. On this journey Walton is accompanied by Old Testament scholar Tremper Longman and geologist Steve Moshier. As in earlier ventures into Lost Worlds, Longman and Walton, bolstered by an evangelical high view of Scripture, set forth their findings in a series of propositions. In their interpretations of the Genesis flood narrative as well as the narratives of the sons of God and the tower of Babel, they apply insights from the ancient Near Eastern cultural context, which, they maintain, was common to both Israel and its neighbors. They conclude that the overarching theme of non-order, order, and disorder in relation to the divine presence is at the heart of the narratives. In essence, these familiar stories were rooted in actual, historical events, such as a significant local flood, but described in figurative language entailing hyperbole to make significant theological points about God's presence. The authors insist that the narratives were not intended to provide information with which to reconstruct the historical events themselves. In support of that contention, Moshier provides a geological critique of flood geology, the view that Genesis teaches a yearlong, worldwide flood that deposited most of Earth's fossiliferous strata. *The Lost World of the Flood* is a must-read for all fans of the Lost World books, especially those who are trying to understand Genesis 1–11 in the context of modern science. This book is a treasury of creative, thought-provoking proposals and insights, and is a pleasure to read."

Davis A. Young, emeritus professor of geology, Calvin College

"Many readers of the Bible are perplexed about how to understand the seemingly legendary stories in Genesis 1–11. In continuity with Walton's previous Lost World books, Longman and Walton—both of whom have written commentaries on Genesis—provide astute guidance for reading the flood narrative as part of the larger story of Genesis 1–11 and in the context of other ancient Near Eastern literature. Attentive to contemporary questions of science and history that many readers bring to the text, they zero in on the sort of literature the flood story is, helping us to better understand its theological claims, which are meant to impact human life both in ancient times and today."

J. Richard Middleton, professor of biblical worldview and exegesis, Northeastern Seminary at Roberts Wesleyan College

THE
LOST WORLD
OF THE
FLOOD

Mythology, Theology, and
the Deluge Debate

TREMPER LONGMAN III
& JOHN H. WALTON

With a contribution by Stephen O. Moshier

IVP Academic

An imprint of InterVarsity Press
Downers Grove, Illinois

InterVarsity Press
P.O. Box 1400, Downers Grove, IL 60515-1426
ivpress.com
email@ivpress.com

InterVarsity Press® is the book-publishing division of InterVarsity Christian Fellowship/USA®, a movement of students and faculty active on campus at hundreds of universities, colleges, and schools of nursing in the United States of America, and a member movement of the International Fellowship of Evangelical Students. For information about local and regional activities, visit intervarsity.org.

All Scripture quotations, unless otherwise indicated, are taken from The Holy Bible, New International Version®, NIV®. Copyright © 1973, 1978, 1984, 2011 by Biblica, Inc.™ Used by permission of Zondervan. All rights reserved worldwide. www.zondervan.com. The "NIV" and "New International Version" are trademarks registered in the United States Patent and Trademark Office by Biblica, Inc.™

Cover design: Cindy Kiple
Interior design: Daniel van Loon
Image: Flood, ©2009 by Paul Powis / Private Collection / Bridgeman Images

ISBN 978-0-8308-5200-0 (print)
ISBN 978-0-8308-8782-8 (digital)

Printed in the United States of America ∞

InterVarsity Press is committed to ecological stewardship and to the conservation of natural resources in all our operations. This book was printed using sustainably sourced paper.

Library of Congress Cataloging-in-Publication Data

Names: Longman, Tremper, author. | Walton, John H., 1952- author.
Title: The lost world of the flood : mythology, theology, and the deluge
    debate / Tremper Longman III and John H. Walton ; with a contribution by
    Stephen Moshier.
Description: Downers Grove : InterVarsity Press, 2018. | Includes index.
Identifiers: LCCN 2018011458 (print) | LCCN 2018012610 (ebook) | ISBN
    9780830887828 (eBook) | ISBN 9780830852000 (pbk. : alk. paper)
Subjects: LCSH: Deluge. | Bible. Genesis, I-XI--Criticism, interpretation,
    etc.
Classification: LCC BS658 (ebook) | LCC BS658 .L66 2018 (print) | DDC
    222/.1106—dc23
LC record available at https://lccn.loc.gov/2018011458

P	20	19	18	17	16	15	14	13	12	11	10	9	8	7	6	5	4	3
Y	36	35	34	33	32	31	30	29	28	27	26	25	24	23	22	21	20	19

Contents

PART 4. THE WORLD: THINKING ABOUT EVIDENCE FOR THE FLOOD

Preface

Four previous works in the Lost World series have established its underlying concepts:

- Accessible discussion of a topic of current popular (not just academic) interest
- Addressed through propositions that move the reader through a logical sequence of the principal points of discussion
- Based on a fresh, close reading of the Hebrew text
- Informed by knowledge of the ancient Near Eastern literature and cognitive environment
- Undergirded by a consistently applied hermeneutic that finds God's authoritative message in the text represented in the communication as understood by the human source (speaker or writer) and his audience—working out the principle that the Bible is written for us, but not to us

The account of the flood (situated in the context of Genesis 1–11) is inarguably an excellent candidate for such a study. It provides an example of a text that has been subjected to many modern readings as interpreters focus on apologetics and scientific and historical reconstruction of the event. We will argue that these not only miss the point but potentially distort the biblical message.

The issues the Lost World books deal with are inherently controversial—that is why they remain issues of debate. Consequently, any treatment of them will be controversial, as this one will be. For open-minded readers who are seeking an interpretation that will make sense to them, we invite you to plunge in and engage the options we have proposed.

As always in the Lost World books, the intention is not to offer the single "correct" interpretation of the text. We seek, instead, to provide an interpretation based on a conviction that the Bible is the Word of God—Scripture that speaks truly. At the same time we recognize the importance of genre, of an understanding of the ancient world, and of the importance of a sound hermeneutic for arriving at an understanding of that truth. Our goal is not to convert the reader to our conclusions, or even to persuade the reader to adopt our way of thinking. Instead, we seek to bring information to the reader's attention that has helped us as we have struggled with the passages. If readers deem that information useful and beneficial, we are gratified. But for readers who cannot accept our findings, believing that Scripture makes claims that require other conclusions, we hope that at least we have shown how our particular interpretation is the result of faithful interpretation.

Abbreviations

AfO	*Archiv für Orientforschung*
ANE	ancient Near East(ern)
ANET	*Ancient Near Eastern Texts Relating to the Old Testament.* Edited by James B. Pritchard. 3rd ed. Princeton, NJ: Princeton University Press, 1969.
BSac	*Bibliotheca Sacra*
BSOT	*Behind the Scenes of the Old Testament.* Edited by Jonathan Greer, John Hilber, and John Walton. Grand Rapids: Baker, forthcoming.
CAD	*The Assyrian Dictionary of the Oriental Institute of the University of Chicago.* 21 vols. Chicago: Oriental Institute of Chicago, 1956–2006.
COS	*The Context of Scripture.* Edited by William W. Hallo. 3 vols. Leiden: Brill, 1997–2002.
EI	*Eretz Israel*
FOTL	Forms of the Old Testament Literature
IDB	*The Interpreter's Dictionary of the Bible.* Edited by George A. Buttrick. 4 vols. New York: Abingdon, 1962.
JBL	*Journal of Biblical Literature*
JNES	*Journal of Near Eastern Studies*
JSOT	*Journal for the Study of the Old Testament*
NICOT	New International Commentary on the Old Testament
NIVAC	NIV Application Commentary

NT	New Testament
OBO	Orbis Biblicus et Orientalis
OT	Old Testament
RAI	Recontre assyriologique internationale
RIME	The Royal Inscriptions of Mesopotamia, Early Periods
SGBC	Story of God Bible Commentary
TynBul	*Tyndale Bulletin*
WBC	Word Biblical Commentary
ZAW	*Zeitschrift für die alttestamentliche Wissenschaft*

PART 1

METHOD:
PERSPECTIVES ON
INTERPRETATION

Genesis Is an Ancient Document

We all desire to be faithful interpreters of God's Word to assure that we receive the full benefit of God's revelation to us. We consider the Bible to have authority, and we want to submit ourselves and our lives to that authority. Biblical authority is tied inseparably to the author's intention. God vested his authority in a human author, so we must consider what the human author intended to communicate if we want to understand what God's message is. Two voices speak: the human author is our doorway into the room of God's meaning and message. Thus, when we read Genesis we are reading an ancient document and should begin by using only the assumptions that would be appropriate for the ancient world. We must understand how the ancients thought and what ideas underlay their communication.

Even though we may rarely identify a passage of the Bible that could be arguably indebted to specific awareness of a known text from the ancient Near East, for the most part we are interested in understanding how Israel in the Old Testament was embedded in the ancient world. Whether the revelation of God in the Old Testament reflects the kind of thinking that was common throughout the ancient world or it exhorts the Israelites to abandon the standard thinking in the ancient world, the conversation that takes place in the Bible is assuredly situated in the ancient world. So the more we can learn about the ancient world, the more faithful our interpretation will be.

In one sense, every successful act of communication is accomplished by various degrees of accommodation on the part of the communicator, but only for the sake of the audience they have in mind. Accommodation must bridge the gap when communicator and audience do not share the same language, the same command of language, the same culture, or the same experiences, but we do not expect a communicator to accommodate an audience they do not know or anticipate. *High context* communication takes place between insiders in situations in which the communicator and audience share much in common. In such situations, less accommodation is necessary for effective communication to take place, and therefore much might be left unsaid that an outsider might need in order to fully understand the communication.

This is illustrated in the traffic reports that we hear in Chicago, where the references to times of travel and location of problems assume the listener has an intimate understanding of the highways. Traffic reports that offer times of travel from various identified points and stretches where one might encounter congestion are very meaningful to me (John) as a regular commuter. I know exactly what to expect by a report that it will take thirty-eight minutes to drive from "the Cave" to "the Junction" and that it is congested from "the Slip to the Nagle curve." When out-of-town guests visit, however, this information confuses them. They do not know what the *Slip* or the *Cave* are (nor could they find them on a map); they don't know how far these places are from one another, and they don't know that on a good day one can go from the Cave to the Junction in about eight minutes.

By contrast, in *low context* communication, high levels of accommodation are necessary as an insider attempts communication with an outsider. A low context traffic report would have to explain to out-of-town listeners or inexperienced commuters just where the different locations are and what normal times look like from one lo-cation to another. These would be much longer reports. If the traffic reporter made the report understandable to the out-of-town visitor, it would be too tiring to be of any use to the regular commuter.

We propose that in the Bible, a human communicator is engaged in expressing an accommodating message to a high context (i.e., ancient Israelite) audience. So, for example, a prophet and his audience share a history, a culture, a language, and the experiences of their contem-poraneous lives. God has employed this communication as his reve-lation of his plan and purposes. When we read the Bible, we enter the context of that communication as low context outsiders who need to use all of our inferential tools to discern the nature of the communi-cation that takes place in that ancient setting, as well as discern from that the revelation God has offered through that communication. We have to use research to fill in all the information that would not have to be said by the prophet in his high context communication to his audience. This is how we, as modern readers, must interact with an ancient text.

Those who take the Bible seriously believe God has inspired the locutions (words, whether spoken or written) the communicator has used to accomplish joint (divine and human authors) illocutions (which lead to an understanding of intentions, claims, affirmations, and, ultimately, meaning), but that the foundational locutions are tied to the communicator's world.[1] Whatever the human communicator's illocution is, God has added a second illocution (revelation) to that. Inspiration is tied to *locutions* (they have their source in God); *illocu-tions* define the necessary path to meaning that can be defined as char-acterized by authority.

At times our distance from the ancient communicator might mean that we misunderstand the communication because of elements

---

[1] Illocutions are the focus of the speech-act (e.g., promise, command, blessing, instruction). The illocution identifies what communicators are doing with their words.

foreign to us or because we do not share ways of thinking with the communicator. Comparative studies help us to understand more fully the form of the biblical authors' employed genres and the nature of their rhetorical devices so we do not mistake these elements for something they never were. Such an exercise does not compromise the authority of Scripture but ascribes authority to that which the communicator was actually communicating. We also need comparative studies in order to recognize the aspects of the communicators' cognitive environment that are foreign to us, and to read the text in light of their world and worldview. This is not imposing something foreign on the text; it is an attempt to recognize that which is inherent in the text by virtue of its situatedness—the author and audience are embedded in the ancient world. We are not imposing this on the text any more than we are imposing Hebrew on the text when we try to read it in its original language.

We will illustrate by using the metaphor of a cultural river. In our modern world the cultural river is easily identified. Among its currents are various fundamentals such as rights, freedom, capitalism, democracy, individualism, globalism, market economy, scientific naturalism, an expanding universe, empiricism, and natural laws, just to name a few. Some may wish to float in these currents, while others may struggle to swim upstream against them, but everyone in our modern world inevitably is located in its waters. Regardless of our diverse ways of thinking, we are all in the cultural river, and its currents are familiar to us.

In the ancient world a very different cultural river flowed through all of the diverse cultures: Egyptian, Phoenician, Assyrian—or Israelite. Despite variations between cultures and across the centuries, certain elements remained largely static. Continual course adjustments have little effect on the most persistent currents. People are people, but few of the currents common to the ancient cultures are found in our modern cultural river. In the ancient cultural river we would find currents such as community identity, the comprehensive and ubiquitous control of the gods, the role of kingship, divination, the centrality of the temple, the mediatory role of images, and the reality of the spirit world and magic.

The Israelites sometimes floated on the currents of that cultural river without resistance, and we should be neither surprised nor critical. At other times, however, the revelation of God encouraged them to struggle out of the current into the shallows, or even to swim furiously upstream. Whatever the extent of the Israelites' interactions with the cultural river, it is important to remember that they were situated in the *ancient* cultural river, not immersed in the currents of our modern cultural river.

We seek to understand this embeddedness so we may be faithful interpreters of the biblical text. God communicated within the context of their cultural river. God's message, God's purposes, and God's authority were all vested in Israelite communicators for Israelite audiences, and the message took shape according to the internal logic within their language and culture. We cannot be assured of authoritative communication through any other source. We must therefore find the message of God as communicated through those intermediaries in their ancient cultural river.

If we are to interpret Scripture to receive the full impact of God's authoritative message, and build the foundation for sound theology, we have to begin by leaving our cultural river behind, with all our modern issues and perspectives, to understand the cultural river of the ancient intermediaries. The communicators that we encounter in the Old Testament are not aware of our cultural river—including all of its scientific aspects; they neither address our cultural river nor anticipate it. We cannot therefore assume that any of the constants or currents of our cultural river are addressed in Scripture.

Consequently, we are obliged to respect the text by recognizing the sort of text it is and the nature of the message it offers. In that regard, we have long recognized that the Bible is not a scientific textbook addressing issues from our modern vantage point. That is, God's intention is not to teach about the scientific aspects of events or phenomena. He *does* reveal his work in the world, but he *doesn't* reveal how the world works.

As an example of the foreign aspects of the cognitive environment, people in the ancient world had no category for what we call natural laws. When they thought of cause and effect, even though they could make all the observations we make (e.g., when you push something it moves; when you drop something it falls), they were more inclined to see the world's operations in terms of divine agency. Everything worked the way it did because God set it up that way and God maintained the system. They would not have viewed the cosmos as a machine but as a kingdom, and God communicated to them about the world in those terms. His revelation was not focused on giving them a more sophisticated understanding of the mechanics of the natural world.

He likewise did not hide information of that sort in the text for later readers to discover. An assumption on our part that he did would have no reliable controls. For example, in the days when we believed in a steady-state universe, people could easily have gone to the Bible to find confirmation of that science. But today we no longer believe steady-state to be true. Today we might think we find confirmation of the big bang or the expanding universe, but someday we may no longer consider those to be true. Such approaches cannot be adopted within an authority framework.

In the same way, the authority of the text is not respected when statements in the Bible that are part of ancient science are used as if they are God's descriptions of modern scientific understanding.[2] When the text talks about thinking with our hearts or intestines, it is

---

[2]See discussion on this point in Kenneth Keathley, J. B. Stump, and Joe Aguirre, eds., *Old-Earth or Evolutionary Creation?* (Downers Grove, IL: InterVarsity Press, 2017), 27-48.

not proposing scientific ideas we must confirm if we wish to take biblical authority seriously. We need not try to propose ways that our blood-pumping organs or digestive systems are physiologically involved in cognitive processes. This is simply communication in the context of ancient science. In the same way, when the text talks about "waters above," we do not have to construct a cosmic system that has waters above. Everyone in the ancient world believed in a cosmic ocean suspended above a solid sky. Therefore, when the biblical text talks about "waters above" it is not offering authoritative revelation of scientific facts. If we conclude that there are not, strictly speaking, waters above, we have not thereby identified an error in Scripture. Rather, we have recognized that God vests the authority of the text elsewhere. Authority is tied to the message the author intends to communicate as an agent of God's revelation. This communication by God initiates that revelation by piggybacking on communication by a human addressing the world of ancient Israel. Even though the Bible is written *for* us, it is not written *to* us. The revelation it provides can equip us to know God, his plan, and his purposes, and therefore to participate with him in the world we face today. But it was not written with our world in mind. In its context, it is not communicated in our language; it is not addressed to our culture; it does not anticipate the questions about the world and its operations that stem from our modern situations and issues.

If we read modern ideas into the text, we skirt the authority of the text and in effect are compromising it. The result would be to arrogate authority to ourselves and our ideas. The text cannot mean what it never meant. What the text says may converge with modern science, but the text does not make authoritative claims pertaining to modern science (e.g., some statements may coincide with big bang cosmology, but the text does not authoritatively establish big bang cosmology). What the author meant and what the audience understood places restrictions on what has authority. The only way we can move with certainty beyond the Old Testament author's intention is if another authoritative voice (e.g., a New Testament author) gives us that extension of meaning.

We propose instead that our doctrinal affirmations about Scripture (authority, inerrancy, infallibility, etc.) attach to the intended message of the human communicator (as it was employed by the divine communicator). This is not to say that we therefore believe everything he believes (he *did* believe that there was a solid sky), but we express our commitment to his communicative act. Since the form of his message is grounded in his language and culture, it is important to differentiate between what the communicator can be inferred to believe and the focus of his intended teaching.[3] The idea that people think with their entrails is built into the expressions that they use and the beliefs of the biblical communicators, but the revelatory intention is not to make assertions about physiology or anatomy. To set aside such culturally bound ideas does not jeopardize the text's message or authority. Genre is also part of the communication framework and is therefore culturally bound. We have to account for the cultural aspects and shape of the genre before we can properly understand the communicator's intentions.[4] At the other end of the spectrum, having once understood the message, we cannot bypass it to adopt only a generalized application (e.g., "love God and your neighbor, and you will do fine") that dismisses as accommodation and potentially erroneous the communicator's genre-encased message.

The authority and inerrancy of the text is, and has traditionally been, attached to what it affirms. Those affirmations are not of a

---

[3]Even Jerome recognized this distinction when he notes, "Many things in Sacred Scripture . . . are said in accordance with the opinion of the time in which the events took place, rather than in accordance with the actual truth of the matter." Jerome, *Commentary on Jeremiah* 28:10-11. I am grateful to Michael Graves for this reference.

[4]A technique illustrated in K. Lawson Younger Jr., *Ancient Conquest Accounts* (Sheffield, UK: JSOT Press, 1990); and John H. Walton, *Lost World of Genesis One* (Downers Grove, IL: InterVarsity Press, 2009).

scientific nature. The text does not affirm that we think with our entrails (though it communicates in those terms because that is what the ancient audience believed). The text does not affirm that there are waters above (i.e., a cosmic ocean held up by a solid sky). The question we must therefore address is whether the text, in its authority, makes any affirmations about the extent and nature of the flood as a scientist today would think about it. If the communication of the text adopts the "science" and the ideas that everyone in the ancient world believed (as it did with physiology and the waters above), then we would want to distinguish their perspectives from the authoritative message of the text.

Here is how this paradigm works. First, there is a real world, but the Bible does not *describe* that world authoritatively. Its description is both culturally conditioned (solid sky, waters above, etc.) and rhetorically shaped. We cannot derive a scientific explanation of the world from the Bible, and it would be misguided to try to find scientific evidence for that description. Nevertheless, the Bible does *interpret* that world authoritatively (God's work in it and relationship to it).

We can apply that same paradigm to the flood. There was a real, cataclysmic event, but the Bible does not *describe* that event authoritatively. Its description is culturally conditioned (the flood tradition we all know) and rhetorically shaped (universalistic cosmic proportions). We cannot derive a scientific explanation of the flood from the Bible, and it would be misguided to try to find scientific evidence for that description. Nevertheless, the Bible does *interpret* that event authoritatively (what God was doing; why it happened: judgment, re-creation, nonorder as response to disorder, covenant, etc.).

This does not preclude the text from reporting historical events that would have involved science that the ancients did not understand (e.g., the mechanics of the flood). In such cases, the Bible is not *providing* scientific revelation; it is being *silent* on scientific matters. Whatever scientific explanations we might posit would not carry the authority of the text (just as our interpretations do not carry authority). In the Bible, we expect to find an authoritative interpretation of an event like the flood, not to be able to reconstruct an authoritative scientific account of the flood. The biblical account has a real event in a real past as its referent, but the revelation of God is not the event, but the interpretation of the event (more about this in proposition fourteen).

We can begin to understand the claims of the text as an ancient document by first paying close attention to what the text says and doesn't say. It is too easy to make intrusive assumptions based on our own culture, cognitive environment, traditions, or questions (i.e., our cultural river). It takes a degree of discipline as readers who are outsiders not to assume our modern perspectives and impose them on the text, but often we do not know we are doing it because our own context is so intrinsic to our thinking and the ancient world is an unknown. The best path to recognizing the distinctions between ancient and modern thinking is to begin paying attention to the ancient world. This is accomplished by immersion in the literature of the ancient world. This by no means supersedes Scripture, but it can be a tool for understanding Scripture. When we are trying to understand the opening chapters of Genesis, our immersion is not limited to the cosmology texts or flood accounts of the ancient world. The clues to cognitive environment can be pieced together from a wide variety of ancient literature. Obviously, not everyone can undertake this task, just as not everyone can take the necessary years to master Hebrew and Greek. Those who have the gifts, calling, and passion for the original languages and the opportunity to study, research, and write use their expertise for the benefit of those who do not. In the same way, those who have the gifts, calling, and passion for the study of the ancient world and the opportunity to research and write can use their expertise for the benefit of those who do not.

Such study is not a violation of the clarity (perspicuity) of Scripture propagated by the Reformers. They were not arguing that every part of Scripture was transparent to any casual reader. If they believed that, they would not have had to write hundreds of volumes trying to explain the complexities of interpretation at both exegetical and theological levels. They were instead trying to make the case that there *is* a plain sense of Scripture that is not esoteric, mystical, or allegorical, and could only be spiritually discerned. Everyone could have access to this plain sense (see reference to the Westminster Confession of Faith in proposition seventeen).

Throughout most of history, scholars have not had access to the information from the ancient world and therefore could not use it to inform their interpretation. Even the early Christian writers were interested in accessing the ancient world (as indicated from their frequent reference to Berossus, a Babylonian priest in the third century BC) but had very limited resources. However, since the beginning of the massive archaeological undertakings in Iraq from the middle of the nineteenth century, more than one million cuneiform texts have been excavated that expose the ancient literature through which we can gain important new insight into the ancient world. This is what provides the basis for our interpretation of the early chapters of Genesis as an ancient document.

In trying to engage Genesis as ancient literature, we do not want to dismiss the insights of interpreters who have populated the history of the church. At the same time, we recognize that those interpreters have hardly been univocal. It is true that the creeds and councils have offered their conclusions about the key theological issues, and those conclusions have often become the consensus of modern doctrine. Yet it has not been the practice of interpreters to disdain fresh attempts to exegete the early chapters on Genesis just because their forebears had arrived at their various conclusions. Martin Luther begins his first chapter on Genesis claiming that "until now there has not been anyone in the church either who has explained everything in the chapter with adequate skill."[5] We should therefore not be dissuaded from seeking fresh knowledge that may lead to reinterpretation, for when we do so we are following in the footsteps of those interpreters who have gone before us, even as we stand on their shoulders.

---

[5]See discussion in Theo M. M. A. C. Bell, "Humanity Is a Microcosm: Adam and Eve in Luther's Lectures on Genesis (1534–45)," in *Out of Paradise: Eve and Adam and Their Interpreters*, ed. B. Becking and S. Hennecke (Sheffield, UK: Phoenix Sheffield, 2011), 67-89.

Proposition 2

Genesis 1–11 Makes Claims
About Real Events in a Real Past

Our purpose in this volume is to come to an understanding of the proper interpretation of the story of the flood in Genesis 6–9. That includes whether it is describing a worldwide deluge, a local flood, or something else, but the extent of the flood is not the most important issue. Since we are seeking first and foremost the literary-theological interpretation offered by the text, we begin with the broader literary context of the flood story—namely, Genesis 1–11. Before dealing with the individual narratives, we will address the larger issue of whether the author or compiler of these chapters intended readers to take them as referring to events that happened in space and time.

The question we want to answer is whether Genesis 1–11 (which includes the flood story) makes historical claims.[1] This investigation involves the identification of the genre or literary type of these chapters in the context of the whole book of Genesis. What reason do

---

[1]There is some risk when using the term *historical*—that readers will immediately bring to mind all that is involved in writing about history in our modern world. In the ancient world they wrote about events differently than we do. The term *history* in this book refers to the basic idea that the literature in the text is using a real event in a real past as the referent for the narrative.

we have to think that the author of Genesis intended to tell us about real past events?

Let's begin with the assumption, not often disputed, that the author intends readers (ancient and modern) to take the ancestor narratives and the Joseph story as history.[2] The question then is whether Genesis 1–11 also intends to tell the reader about actual past events. Due to the difference in style between these opening chapters and the rest of Genesis, such continuity has often been disputed. Genesis 1–11 has often been called poetry, parable, or even myth.[3]

An important point of continuity, however, is found in the *toledot* formula that stretches across the whole of Genesis. *Toledot* is a Hebrew word that is rendered something like "account" in our English translations. The word occurs in a formula that can be translated something like "This is the account of X," where X is, with the exception of the first occurrence, a personal name. These formulas are best understood as referencing written (see Gen 5:1) or oral documents that the author of Genesis used to compile the book. After all, even if Moses is the author of Genesis, he would have used earlier sources to talk about the distant past. We should further note that the "*toledot* of X" is about the offspring of X. So the *toledot* of Terah (Gen 11:27) introduces the story of Abraham, Terah's son (Gen 11:27–25:11).

The first *toledot* occurs in Genesis 2:4 and then occurs ten more times, four times in the rest of Genesis 1–11 (Gen 5:1; 6:9 [the *toledot* of Noah]; 10:1; 11:10) and six times in the rest of the book (Gen 11:27; 25:12, 19; 36:1, 9; 37:2). In other words, the *toledot* formula does, in our opinion, show a literary continuity between Genesis 1–11 and Genesis 12–50.

---

[2]That does not necessarily mean it is history as we would write it today, but rather that it intends to be history in the sense of reporting space-and-time events. See John Van Seters, *Prologue to History: The Yahwist as Historian in Genesis* (Louisville, KY: Westminster John Knox, 1992).

[3]George W. Coats, *Genesis with an Introduction to Narrative Literature*, FOTL 1 (Grand Rapids: Eerdmans, 1983), 1-5.

Further, we would say that the *toledot* formula indicates a consistent interest in a carefully selected sequence of past events. The composer incorporates these sources as reports received from the past to create his account of the past. This is true of Genesis 1–11 as much as Genesis 12–50. This conclusion does not necessarily mean that the composer did not shape the *toledot* as he created the text as we know it.

Discussions about the early chapters of Genesis often focus on whether the accounts are mythology or history. It is an important question, but framing it this way may not be the best approach. Today, we often consider the label *mythology* to imply that what is reported is "not real." But in the ancient world, they did not consider what we call their mythology to be not real. To the contrary, they believed their mythology to represent the most important reality—deep reality, which transcends what could be reported in terms of events that have transpired in the strictly human realm. Indeed, they further considered that even the events in the human realm, which we might label *history*, found their greatest significance in aspects of the event that human eyewitnesses could not see—the involvement of the divine hand.

Consequently, we should be hesitant to set a dichotomy between history (equaling "real") and mythology (equaling "not real"). Such thinking is too overburdened with our modern categories to do justice to ancient literature, biblical or otherwise. The deepest reality, that which is most true, must not be constrained by what eyewitnesses can attest or demonstrate to have "actually happened." The accounts in Genesis 1–11 can be affirmed as having real events as their referents, but the events themselves (yes, they happened) find their significance in the interpretation that they are given in the biblical text. That significance is not founded in their historicity but in their theology; not in *what* happened (or even that something *did* happen) but in *why* it happened. What was God doing? That is where the significance is to be found.

Our defenses of historicity can become reductionistic if we become too focused on proving the reality of events rather than on embracing the interpretation of the theological significance being traced by the author. The text has no interest in trying to prove the events took place. They assume they did, as do we. Instead they are offering an interpretation that constitutes the divine-human message that carries the authority of the text. Events are not authoritative; the interpretation of the narrator is.

Having suggested that the narrator intends the reader to believe that Genesis 1–11 has real events as referents, we still need to consider in more detail how Israelites in the ancient world thought about events.

We propose that on several counts they did not think about events the same way we do. In the ancient world they viewed reality with an eye to the metaphysical (spiritual) world, not just through the lens of empiricism. Consequently, the role of the eyewitness was not as highly valued. Seeing events through a lens that included the spiritual world, and not just the human world, meant that categories we might label *mystical* or *mythical* overlapped in indiscernible and inseparable ways with what we call the real world. *Events* in their view therefore consist of more than what we refer to as *history*. Yet, for all of that expanded view, that does not make the view of events any less real to them. They can have events as the referents to a narrative account, yet view the events in a different way than we do. The ancient world as a whole has different ways of knowing than we do.[4] One of the expressions of this is that they do not have a line between

---

[4]Marc Van de Mieroop, *Philosophy Before the Greeks* (Princeton, NJ: Princeton University Press, 2016). See also Gebhard J. Selz, ed., *Empirical Dimension of Ancient Near Eastern Studies* (Wien, Austria: LIT Verlag, 2011), specifically his article "Remarks on the Empirical Foundation and Scholastic Traditions of Early Mesopotamian Acquisition of Knowledge," 49-70. See particularly the following from his conclusion: "The ancient Mesopotamians' attitude towards the acquisition of knowledge was generally founded in their concept of 'empiricism.' The major differences from modern concepts can be attributed to a differing notion of 'realities': in particular, the distinction between first and subsequent orders of realities never gained salience in Mesopotamian thought" (61).

myth and history. Both are involved in events and in reality. To the extent that the Israelites thought in similar ways, they would not distinguish between these ways of knowing. If such is the case, stating that they consider the flood to be a real event is not as clarifying as we might hope. We cannot draw distinctions about narratives that we are interested in if they do not draw their lines in the same places as we do.

When we talk about events—and more importantly, event reports—it will be helpful to imagine a spectrum between metaphysical and empirical.

Metaphysical ———————————————————— Empirical

Event reports are on a sliding scale. In our modern cultural river, history is considered entirely empirical and, in fact, only the empirical is considered to be real. In turn, apologetics engages the empirical. Event reports found in Genesis 1–11 concern what can be called cosmic events, which means that they are located much more toward the metaphysical end of the spectrum. But unlike what we call myth in the ancient world, which we consider as having no empirical aspect and therefore located at the far end of the metaphysical side of the spectrum, Genesis 1–11 retains some empirical aspects.[5] When we compare that to Genesis 12–50, we find the reports of the events pertaining to the ancestors are pushed quite a bit further along the spectrum toward the empirical side. Even so, the metaphysical remains more important than the empirical. Unlike many in our modern cultural river, we consider the metaphysical aspects just as real as the empirical ones. The more toward one side or the other the event report is located on the spectrum, the less the other aspect can be detected. If the report is

---

[5]Even the use of a spectrum for communicating these ideas is misleading because in the ancient world they would not have distinguished them as opposite poles. They would be fully integrated into one another. The spectrum way of representation is simply for our purposes of explanation.

more interested in the metaphysical, then our analysis of the report ought to be more focused on the metaphysical aspects.

It is not so important precisely where we locate a report on the spectrum; however, it is important to realize these two aspects are both part of how they viewed events. It is also important to note that we should not think of the metaphysical aspects and the empirical aspects as adding up to 100 percent, with say 36 percent being one and 64 percent being the other. These categories cannot be distinguished as exclusive of one another.

Consequently, even as we affirm that the author envisioned these accounts as real events in a real past, we recognize that they would have viewed events and reality differently and therefore would have provided testimony that is different from how we would do it.[6] Their testimony is predominantly interested in the metaphysical aspects.[7] This is particularly true of cosmic events such as the flood. This needs to be kept in mind as we decide what should be the most appropriate focus of our textual analysis.

---

[6]A similar point has been made concerning iconography. "The ANE created conceptual rather than perceptual images. It is not so much a matter of what is seen, but of what the viewer is supposed to see or perceive—a notion or symbol that was communicated or supposed to be communicated. Images are neither always realistic nor historical in the sense of representing reality. It is not a case of what some ruler or historical person really looked like or what really happened that matters, but (for example) the 'idea' of kingship that is communicated. This is important, as it means that iconography provides information on the *world of ideas* of the ANE." I. Cornelius, "An Introduction to Ancient Near Eastern Iconography," in *BSOT*.

[7]Consider how this was so even in more recent history—for example, the way the accounts of the events surrounding Joan of Arc integrate the aspects of the battles and her visions. Even in the twenty-first century, vestiges of this thinking remain. When a massive tsunami struck Indonesia in 2004, killing tens of thousands, the photographs in the aftermath showed totally devastated areas where only the mosques remained (people had found refuge there). Faithful Muslims are not persuaded that the mosques survived because they were of more sturdy construction. They are convinced that Allah spared the mosques and the people in them. For them, the empirical is tempered by the metaphysical. Edward Harris, "Sturdy Mosques Survived Tsunami," *Seattle Times*, January 14, 2005, www.seattletimes.com/nation-world/sturdy-mosques-survived-tsunami.

Genesis 1–11 Uses Rhetorical Devices

In previous propositions we explored what signaled to the reader that Genesis 1–11, beginning with creation and fall, consists of actual space-and-time events. In other words, the author intends the reader to understand that he is writing about the real past.

We have also noted, however, that there are clear signals that the writing, while referential, is not particularly interested in *reporting* the event in a way that allows us to *reconstruct* the event, but rather focuses on the *interpretation* of the event. In other words, the author depicts the event in a way that furthers his theological message.

This observation is not just true of Genesis 1–11 but all biblical history—indeed, all history. Writing about events, *history*, is always interpretive, giving us the author's perspective on the event through selection and emphasis. The writing does not necessarily bring us back to a complete or impartial understanding of the event itself. We can gain an adequate knowledge of the event that motivates the telling of the event, but not in some kind of value-neutral or brute-fact manner.

All history writing is rhetorically shaped. Authors cannot be exhaustive in their telling of the event, so they choose what is important or, better stated, what they think is important about the event. Thus, authors provide the perspective through which we hear or read about the event.

Furthermore, they tell the story out of their worldview, which is why biblical scholars who work within the framework of the historical-critical method cannot endorse the depiction of the past offered by the biblical historians. After all, historical criticism operates with perspectives that immediately disqualify the supernatural worldview of the biblical authors, who recount the past with a robust awareness of God's involvement in the world. Perhaps the commitment of historical criticism most devastating to the biblical worldview is the principle of analogy, which requires that the historian can treat as plausible in the past only those events that conform with present experience.[1] Thus, we reject the historical-critical approach to the flood story because it does not honor the fact that the story is told from the worldview of the biblical authors. We are more inclined to agree with Ziony Zevit, who insists that some qualification is needed regarding how skepticism (characteristic of the historical-critical approach) can be wielded as a historical hermeneutic. He instead calls for an approach that the major test should be deniability. That is, "whatever is not effectively denied or disproved is to be regarded as true."[2]

Biblical narrators thus speak from their worldview and select and emphasize aspects of the past that communicate their interest in God and the relationship between God and his human creatures. For this reason it is appropriate to refer to those biblical books that look to the past as theological histories.

---

[1] As John J. Collins points out in *The Bible After Babel: Historical Criticism in a Postmodern Age* (Grand Rapids: Eerdmans, 2005), modern historical criticism, his own approach, is built on the history of philosophy presented by Ernst Troeltsch ("Über historische und dogmatische Methode in der Theologie," in *Gesammelte Schriften* [Tübingen: Mohr, 1913]). In English, see "Historiography," in *Encyclopedia of Religion and Ethics*, ed. James Hastings et al. (New York: Scribner's, 1914), 6:716-23.

[2] Ziony Zevit, *Religions of Ancient Israel* (London: Continuum, 2001), 78-79. It should be noted that Zevit is quoting from Leona Toker, "Toward a Poetics of Documentary Prose—From the Perspective of Gulag Testimonies," *Poetics Today* 18 (1997): 190-92, 194. Also, in fairness, it is likely that Zevit would not consider the flood account to be in the same category as the historical testimony he was discussing.

Furthermore, historians, including biblical writers about the past, do more than simply report events (just the facts); they interpret the significance of the events. Indeed, again, biblical authors are not interested in giving us what we need to recreate the event in its pure facticity but rather in using the event to communicate their theological message. It is their theological message that carries the authority God has vested in them. Events are not inspired; interpretations of events are inspired. That the biblical authors are giving us a selective and interpretive accounting of the past to present their theological message is well confirmed by the following quote by the Gospel writer: "Jesus performed many other signs in the presence of his disciples, which are not recorded in this book. But these are written that you may believe that Jesus is the Messiah, the Son of God, and that by believing you may have life in his name" (Jn 20:30-31).

Let's use the report concerning Jesus' speech as a New Testament example. Both Matthew and Luke report a sermon Jesus gave that includes a section we know as the Beatitudes as well as teaching on loving one's enemies, not judging others, the tree and its fruit, and the wise and foolish builders (compare Mt 5-7 with Lk 6:17-49). The teaching in Matthew is much more extensive than Luke's, and there are other differences, but we will illustrate our point with a detail concerning the setting of the sermon.

Whereas Jesus delivered this sermon "on a level place" in Luke 6:17, according to Matthew, Jesus spoke "on a mountainside" (Mt 5:1). Can we reconstruct the actual setting of this sermon? Well, we can speculate, but we cannot be certain. Some believe Jesus spoke on a level spot on a mountain. Maybe. But again, we cannot with certainty re-create the historical event behind the text, though we are right to say that there was a historical event behind the text.

What is more important is the theological message communicated by this rhetorically shaped presentation of the historical event. What is the significance of the place where Jesus spoke the sermon? We can

identify the theological purpose of Matthew quite easily once we remember that he directs his Gospel at Jewish Christian readers. The
location of the Sermon on the Mount, as we have come to refer to it,
contributes to the presentation of Jesus as the fulfillment of the exodus.[3] After having been baptized in the Jordan River (his Red Sea
crossing) and being tempted in the wilderness for forty days and forty
nights (as the Israelites spent forty years in the wilderness), Jesus then
picked twelve disciples (reflecting the twelve tribes of Israel), and then
delivered the Sermon on the Mount, where he spoke about the law. No
Jewish Christian could miss it. Jesus on a mountain talking about the
law would make them think of God giving the law to Moses on Mount
Sinai. Parallels with the exodus continue and culminate in Jesus' cru-
cifixion on the eve of the Passover, the annual celebration of the exodus.

With this background in mind, we now return to Genesis 1–11,
where we are particularly struck by the pervasive and intense use of
figurative language used in the depiction of the past. When we speak
of language as *figurative* we are including the author's intentional use
of rhetorical and literary devices such as metaphor and hyperbole to
get his point across. We believe and advocate for the understanding
that a truly literal reading of Genesis 1–11, or any narrative, recognizes
figurative language when it is intended by the author. We will tend to
avoid the language of *literal* versus *nonliteral* because some people
believe a literal reading does not honor figurative or metaphorical
language as figurative or metaphorical, but rather reads in a nonfigurative manner. We do not think such readings are literal but are simply
wrong in that they do not take the language in the way that the author
intended us to receive it.

How do we know when an author intends to be figurative? It is not
always easy, but sometimes a strong case can be put forward that the
most natural reading of a particular passage is clearly figurative. We

---

[3]Tremper Longman III, *How to Read Exodus* (Downers Grove, IL: InterVarsity Press, 2009), 145-55.

can tell such a reading is the most natural because we have to work hard to take it any other way.

Psalm 23, for instance, begins "The LORD is my shepherd." Everyone to my knowledge understands this statement as figurative, in this case a metaphorical depiction of God as one who protects, guides, and provides for his people. Consequently, a literal interpretation understands this statement as a metaphor. Why? Because the psalmist was not a sheep but a human being. God acts toward the psalmist as a shepherd acts toward a sheep.

Is there any obviously figurative language in Genesis 1–11? First, we should say that there are a number of items that almost everyone would agree are figurative. A partial list would include the description of animals coming forth from the ground (Gen 2:19), the description that God "opened" the eyes of Adam and Eve (Gen 3:7), and God's claim to Cain that Abel's blood was crying out from the ground (Gen 4:10).

But we believe other more debated features of the stories are rhetorically shaped and not presented so readers can reconstruct events that have happened in the past. These we can discern as rhetorically shaped by how hard interpreters who deny that the language is figurative have to work to provide a nonfigurative reading of the narrative.

Let's take an example that has been obvious to most since the early periods of the history of interpretation but denied by so-called young earth creationists—namely, the days of Genesis 1. There is no doubt but that the creation is described as a normal six-day work week with a day of rest, but there are also signals that the author does not intend for us to use this to reconstruct an actual weeklong creation process. Indeed, the rhetorical shaping helps us see that the creation account is not presenting an account of material origins but rather equating to the seven days of temple inauguration.[4]

---

[4]This is presented at length by John H. Walton, *The Lost World of Genesis One* (Downers Grove, IL: InterVarsity Press, 2009).

A literal reading of Genesis 1 should immediately convince readers that the six days of creation are not meant to be understood as twenty-four-hour days with actual evenings and mornings. After all, the sun, moon, and stars do not come into being (or are not made functional) until the fourth day. The early church father Origen observes,

> To what person of intelligence, I ask, will the account seem logically consistent that says there was a "first day" and a "second day" and a "third day," in which also "evening" and "morning" are named, without a sun, without a moon, and without stars, and even in the case of the first day without a heaven?

Origen, we will admit, is a bit heavy handed here because actually there are people of intelligence who believe that Genesis 1 describes literal days in spite of the absence of celestial bodies. The problem is they may be too intelligent (or clever) by a half.

A number of rather ingenious explanations have been presented in order to preserve the view that these days describe actual twenty-four-hour periods of God's creation. One view states that God simply used other forms of light (after all, light is brought into existence on day one). In response, we point out that evening and morning are defined by the rising and setting of the sun, not some other hypothetical light source that God flipped on and off in a twenty-four-hour cycle. Another view suggests that the sun, moon, and stars were actually created on day one (part of the light) but that the story is told from the perspective of someone living on the earth and that, though created earlier, these celestial bodies could only be seen for the first time on the fourth day. But why tell the story this way when on the fourth day there are no humans to perceive the sun, moon, and stars anyway?

These are examples of what we mean by "working too hard." It's much more natural to read the days of creation not as an actual week but as a figurative description of creation based on the common work week during the time the Genesis account was written.

Origen, though, does not stop with the days of creation; he goes on to lambast those who would not recognize the figurative language of Genesis 3:

> And who will be found simple enough to believe that like some farmer "God planted trees in the garden of Eden, in the east" and that he planted "the tree of life" in it, that is a visible tree that could be touched, so that someone could eat of this tree with corporeal teeth and gain life, and further, could eat of another tree and receive the knowledge of "good and evil"? Moreover, we find that God is said to stroll in the garden in the afternoon and Adam to hide under the tree. Surely, I think no one doubts that these statements are made by Scripture in the form of a figure by which they point to certain mysteries.[5]

Again, we don't agree with Origen's rather insulting style, but he is certainly correct that the author of Genesis would expect his audience to understand that he is describing a historical event (human rebellion against God that explains the entrance of sin and death into the world, as Paul will later make clear in Rom 5:12-20), but doing so using figurative language.[6]

We would add to Origen's examples a reference to Genesis 2:7: "Then the LORD God formed a man from the dust of the ground and breathed into his nostrils the breath of life, and the man became a living being." Such a description of the creation of the first man is

---

[5] Origen, *On First Principles* 4.3.1, cited and discussed in Conor Cunningham, *Darwin's Pious Idea: Why the Ultra-Darwinists and Creationists Both Get It Wrong* (Grand Rapids: Eerdmans, 2010), 381-82.

[6] My purpose in citing Origen is not to endorse his overall hermeneutical approach, which many evangelical Protestants find objectionable, but to demonstrate that many, though not all, leaders in the early church recognized the figurative nature of the creation account. For those who find Augustine more helpful (including many Reformed Christians, due to his formidable influence on Calvin), we can add him as a witness since he denies that the days of the creation account are "solar days" (Augustine, *The Literal Meaning of Genesis*, 2 vols. [Mahwah, NJ: Paulist, 1982], 154, cited in Cunningham, *Darwin's Pious Idea*, 296).

patently figurative once we realize that God is a spiritual being and does not have lungs.

Could God have taken a human form to do this? I guess so, but why would we think so? Why should we presume that the ancient author has any interest in telling us how God actually did it?

Genesis 1–2 marvelously inform the reader that God created everything, including humanity. The description of the creation of the first man in Genesis 2:7 also makes an important statement about the relationship between humanity, God, and creation itself. The picture of God taking dust to make humans shows that humans are a part of creation. The fact that the narrator describes God as breathing on the dust in order to enliven the human shows our special relationship with God.[7]

While we believe that the obvious figurative language in Genesis 1–11 is sufficient to make our case that the historical events behind the text are rhetorically shaped by the author, we add yet another figurative feature of these chapters that points in the same direction: anachronisms.

An anachronism represents something in a period other than its own—indeed, at a time when it could not exist (such as a WWII movie featuring cell phones or personal computers). The early chapters of Genesis contain a number of obvious anachronisms to everyone but to those who refuse to pay any attention to the evidence we have from the ancient world. An illustrative but not exhaustive list includes the following:

1. the care of domesticated animals occurring in the second generation of humanity (Gen 4:2-5)

2. the construction of the first city in the second generation of humanity (Gen 4:17)

---

[7]See proposition seven, which describes the connection between Genesis 2:7 and ancient Babylonian creation texts that further explain why the biblical author chose this particular description for the creation of the first man.

3. musical instruments in the eighth generation (Gen 4:21)

4. bronze and iron making in the eighth generation (Gen 4:22)

We point out these anachronisms because they suggest that we must remember that real events are being rhetorically shaped for theological reasons. The biblical authors are not interested in describing these events as we might view them in a videotape presentation.

We reserve a specific discussion of the flood narrative's use of figurative language until proposition five. However, our examples from Genesis 1–3 serve the purpose of showing that the primeval history rhetorically shapes the presentation of actual past events for theological purposes. The author is not particularly interested in giving us the data that would allow us to reconstruct the event behind the text in any kind of detail. Rather, the author wants us to understand the theological significance of these events, and he utilizes figurative language that ancient readers did (and modern readers should) recognize.

The Bible Uses Hyperbole
to Describe Historical Events

One of the most important types of figurative language used in the rhetoric of the flood narrative is hyperbole. We will demonstrate that the Bible is not hesitant to describe historical events hyperbolically to produce an effect in the reader in order to make a theological point. The narrative about the flood is certainly not the only example of hyperbole.

The description of the conquest of the Promised Land in Joshua 1–12 is a case in point. Joshua 1–12 pictures a complete and utter conquest of the Promised Land, which would be contradicted in Joshua 13–24 and Judges 1 unless we understand, as the ancient audience would have clearly understood, that Joshua 1–12 presents a hyperbolic account for the purpose of making an important theological point.

After military and especially spiritual preparation, Joshua leads the Israelites into the Promised Land. Though there are temporary setbacks, the narrator tells us that the Israelites found great success on the battlefield thanks to the presence of God, the divine warrior. At the end of the description of several conflicts, we get this summary statement:

So Joshua subdued the whole region, including the hill country, the Negev, the western foothills and the mountain slopes, together with all their kings. He left no survivors. He totally destroyed all who breathed, just as the LORD, the God of Israel, had commanded. Joshua subdued them from Kadesh Barnea to Gaza and from the whole region of Goshen to Gibeon. All these kings and their lands Joshua conquered in one campaign, because the LORD, the God of Israel, fought for Israel. (Josh 10:40-42)

At the end of the next series of conflicts, which the Israelites won with God's help, the narrator gives us another summarizing statement:

So Joshua took this entire land: the hill country, all the Negev, the whole region of Goshen, the western foothills, the Arabah and the mountains of Israel with their foothills, from Mount Halak, which rises toward Seir, to Baal Gad in the Valley of Lebanon below Mount Hermon. He captured all their kings and put them to death. (Josh 11:16-17)

A little later in the chapter the narrator adds, "So Joshua took the entire land, just as the LORD had directed Moses, and he gave it as an inheritance to Israel according to their tribal divisions. Then the land had rest from war" (Josh 11:23). Joshua 12 then gives a lengthy summarizing statement of all the successful warfare both in the Transjordan and the Cisjordan.

If we read Joshua 1–12 as a straightforward, dispassionate report of the wars of Joshua, we would have to conclude that all Canaan was taken by the Israelites and not a single Canaanite survived unless they, like Rahab, came over to the Israelite side.

But all we have to do is turn to the next chapter of Joshua:

When Joshua had grown old, the LORD said to him, "You are now very old, and there are still very large areas of land to be taken over.

"This is the land that remains: all the regions of the Philistines and Geshurites, from the Shihor River on the east of Egypt to the territory of Ekron on the north, all of it counted as Canaanite though held by the five Philistine rulers in Gaza, Ashdod, Ashkelon, Gath and Ekron; the territory of the Avvites on the south; all the land of the Canaanites, from Arah of the Sidonians as far as Aphek and the border of the Amorites; the area of Byblos; and all Lebanon to the east, from Baal Gad below Mount Hermon to Lebo Hamath.

"As for all the inhabitants of the mountain regions from Lebanon to Misrephoth Maim, that is, all the Sidonians, I myself will drive them out before the Israelites." (Josh 13:1-6)

A Bible atlas will show visually that this description encompasses quite a bit of land.[1] Indeed, a rough estimate would place the success level at around 50 percent at the highest. In addition, there were some important cities said to be taken by Israel that remained firmly in the hand of the Canaanites, most notably Jerusalem and Hebron, both of which were named in the list of defeated kings in Joshua 12 (see v. 10).

According to Judges 1, the situation had not changed dramatically even "after the death of Joshua" (Judg 1:1), where we hear that Israel still had not defeated large swaths of Canaanite territory. As a matter of fact, Canaan was not completely subdued until the time of David a number of centuries later. The author is intentionally using universalistic language and intends to convey, rhetorically, that the conquest was complete, but that did not correspond to the actual geographical scope of the conquest, only to the significance of the conquest. Thus it uses hyperbole to make a theological point.

The emphasis on total conquest in Joshua 1–12 and the recognition that much land remains in Joshua 13–24 and Judges 1 leads some

---

[1]See, for instance, Barry J. Beitzel, *The New Moody Atlas of the Bible* (Chicago: Moody Publishers, 2009), maps 42 and 43 (pp. 128-29).

scholars to ask which account is a reliable representation of what actually happened. Most scholars who pose this question answer that the latter is closer to the truth, and the former is an idealized or theologically focused presentation of the conquest. Still others try to find ways to harmonize the two, perhaps by suggesting the land was completely taken but then lost, only presenting the need to be conquered yet again.

But both of these strategies of understanding the relationship of Joshua 1–12 to Joshua 13–24 and Judges 1 are uncalled for when we understand that the biblical historian can use hyperbole for effect in order to communicate an important theological message.[2]

In the first place, we would agree that Joshua 13–24 and Judges 1 give an accurate portrayal of the successes and struggles involved in taking the land. We believe that rather than trying to woodenly harmonize the two accounts, we should recognize that the author of Joshua emphasized accounts of victories and omitted setbacks and defeats in order to celebrate the beginning of the fulfillment of the Abrahamic promise of land. As Marten Woudstra puts it, "An air of joyful optimism pervades the book of Joshua. Its keynote is the fulfillment of the promise made to the forefathers regarding the possession of the land of Canaan."[3]

The conquest narratives, thus, are interested in the successes of the conquest since they showed God was fulfilling his promise made in Genesis 12:1-3 of the land. Centuries had passed since this promise was given, so we might imagine the joy that accompanied these divinely helped victories.

Thus, we have in the conquest and the tribal allotment passages as well as the opening of Judges a treatment of the early days of the Israelites' presence in the land that causes the use of hyperbole in Joshua 1–12 to stand out.

---

[2]See discussion in John H. Walton and J. Harvey Walton, *The Lost World of the Israelite Conquest* (Downers Grove, IL: InterVarsity Press, 2017), 178.

[3]Marten H. Woudstra, *The Book of Joshua*, NICOT (Grand Rapids: Eerdmans, 1981), 32.

Finally, we should also take note of Lawson Younger's important work on the ancient Near Eastern background to the conquest accounts in Joshua. He presents many examples to explore his thesis that hyperbole was an expected feature of battle accounts from Egypt, Assyria, and Babylonia, indeed, throughout Israel's ancient neighborhood.[4] As he puts it, "just like other ancient Near Eastern conquest accounts, the biblical narrative utilizes hyperbolic, stereotyped syntagms to build up the account."[5] Among a number of examples from Egypt, he cites the Gebel Barkal stele of Thutmose III:

> The great army of Mitanni,
> It is overthrown in the twinkling of an eye.
> It has perished completely,
> As though they had never existed [lit. "the end"] of fire.[6]

Or we can add a reference to the Israel stele of Merneptah: "Yanoam is made into non-existence; Israel is wasted, its seed is not."[7]

We recognize that some of our readers will have difficulty with the presence of hyperbole in Scripture, even if it is as obvious as we have seen it to be in a text like Joshua 1–12. But we end with a reminder that the evangelical doctrine of the inerrancy of Scripture affirms the utter truthfulness of Scripture in all that it teaches or affirms. Our point is that the biblical authors sometimes employed hyperbole in their materials in a way that they expected their readers to recognize. In other words, hyperbole is a convention of writing that was used by the ancient authors to make important theological points. That such a view of inerrancy is acceptable to evangelical Protestants can be substantiated by citing the Chicago Statement on Biblical Inerrancy, which is

---

[4]K. Lawson Younger, *Ancient Conquest Accounts: A Study in Ancient Near Eastern and Biblical History Writing* (Sheffield, UK: JSOT Press, 1990), 190-92.

[5]Ibid., 228.

[6]Ibid., 191.

[7]From "The (Israel) Stela of Merneptah," trans. James K. Hoffmeier, *COS* 2:41. Younger, *Ancient Conquest Accounts*, 191, cites the first line about Yanoam.

the banner statement of the doctrine written by leading evangelical theologians and biblical scholars in 1978. In article 13 the document, in a series of affirmations and denials, states:

> We affirm the propriety of using inerrancy as a theological term with reference to the complete truthfulness of Scripture.
>
> We deny that it is proper to evaluate Scripture according to standards of truth and error that are alien to its usage or purpose. We further deny that inerrancy is negated by Biblical phenomena such as a lack of modern technical precision, irregularities of grammar or spelling, observational nature, the reporting of falsehoods, *the use of hyperbole* and round numbers, the topical arrangement of material, variant selections of material in parallel accounts, or the use of free citations.[8]

Thus, we can see the Bible is not at all averse or slow to utilize hyperbole to communicate its important theological message, and the most recent articulation of the doctrine of inerrancy fully recognizes this use and affirms that it in no way compromises the truthfulness of Scripture. There are historical events behind these hyperbolic statements, but it is hard if not impossible to reconstruct these events in detail because the biblical authors are not so interested in the event itself as their significance for God's relationship with his people.

---

[8]"The Chicago Statement on Biblical Inerrancy," accessible at www.bible-researcher.com /chicago1.html. Italics added.

Proposition 5

Genesis Appropriately Presents a Hyperbolic Account of the Flood

Based on the discussion of the rhetorical use of hyperbole evidenced in Scripture in proposition four, we are now ready to apply that to our understanding of the flood. We contend that employing universalistic rhetoric to portray the impact and significance of the flood as a cosmic cataclysm does not mean that the ancient Israelites or the author considered the physical scope or geographical range to be universal. Other uses of universalistic language used rhetorically as hyperbole can be identified in Lamentations 2:22 (where the lament over the Babylonian destruction of Jerusalem indicates that there were no survivors, when we are well aware from the rest of the Old Testament that some were taken into exile and others remained in the land) and a similar discussion of the day of the Lord coming on Jerusalem in Zephaniah 1, which indicates that the destruction would be complete and universal.

It is helpful to compare the discussion of primordial cosmic cataclysm in the flood narrative to what we find in apocalyptic literature, which often portrays future cosmic cataclysm. Both sorts of cataclysm accounts are rhetorically shaped to feature a scope of cosmic proportions. The genre of apocalyptic shows us that a portrait of sociopolitical cataclysm can be rhetorically shaped with cosmic proportions. Being aware of that, we propose that a portrait of natural cataclysm could theoretically also be rhetorically shaped with cosmic proportions, and in fact we find flood terminology being used for both sorts of cataclysms in the literature of the ancient Near East (ANE). Yi Samuel Chen even presents evidence that the Sumerian flood account (natural cataclysm) borrows its language from the "Lament over the Destruction of Sumer and Ur" (sociopolitical cataclysm).[1]

In keeping with our understanding of Genesis 1–11 as a whole (and in particular our previous close study of Genesis 1–3; see proposition three), we expect two things in the presentation of the flood story in Genesis 6–8. First, we expect that the flood story is rooted in an actual event, and, second, we expect that that historical event would be described using figurative language, showing more interest in the theological significance of that event than in giving us the information we need to reconstruct the historical event itself.

In proposition fourteen we will reflect on the event itself, but in this section we will explore its rhetorical shaping. In terms of the flood story, the most pronounced rhetorical feature is clearly hyperbole.

Hyperbole is a form of figurative language. It exaggerates in order to produce an effect or to make a point. Let me (Tremper) give an example from everyday conversation. When my wife picks up my luggage and says, "It weighs a ton" (yes, I tend to pack heavy—it's the books), we both know it does not literally weigh a ton, but she has made her point. She is not lying or misleading me, but I might think she is if I believe she is being literal. Indeed, I would show myself quite obtuse if I responded, "It does not. It weighs seventy pounds, well under a ton!"

In our opinion, hyperbole permeates the account of the flood, beginning with the description of pervasive nonorder. "The LORD saw

---

[1]Yi Samuel Chen, *The Primeval Flood Catastrophe* (Oxford: Oxford University Press, 2013), 204.

how great the wickedness of the human race had become on the earth, and that every inclination of the thoughts of the human heart was only evil all the time" (Gen 6:5). If we take that as a bare statement of fact, then how do we explain "Noah was a righteous man, blameless among the people of his time, and he walked faithfully with God" (Gen 6:9)? Only the most literally minded would take this language to mean that everyone on earth had only evil motives for every act. However, the hyperbole certainly expresses well the fact that evil had reached an unprecedented level and that God was going to act to restore order.

Second, hyperbole explains the dimensions of the ark. As described in Genesis 6:15, the ark is about 450 feet long (300 cubits), 75 feet wide (50 cubits), and 45 feet high (30 cubits).[2] That is one large boat! The dimensions themselves lead us to believe that they are hyperbolic numbers, in other words purposefully exaggerated for rhetorical effect to make a (theological) point. It is hard to imagine ancient readers taking this description as if it referred to an actual boat. There would have been nothing like it or even close to it in the ancient world.

Indeed, it is probably easier for a modern audience to misunderstand the text and take it as if it is describing an actual boat. Certainly that is the case with Ken Ham, a leading young-earth creationist. In July 2016 Ken Ham opened the Ark Encounter, a "life-sized" replica of the ark that people can go on. Ham's stated purpose is to show that a literal ark of these dimensions can be built and can house all the animals necessary to survive the flood. I should point out that Ham, for reasons I am not aware of, builds it even larger than the biblical description (510 feet long, 85 feet wide, and 51 feet high).[3]

Ham has shown that such a massive boat could be built. It may even be seaworthy (though it is built on land in Kentucky). However, if you

---

[2]The conversion is based on the traditional understanding that the cubit (which measures the typical length of a forearm from the tip of the middle finger to the bottom of the elbow) was approximately eighteen inches.

[3]He seems to reckon that a cubit is longer than most scholars today believe.

look at the video of its construction, you will notice the power tools, the cranes, the steel scaffolding that keeps the boat from cracking apart, and the tens if not hundreds of skilled workers with their power tools who built this boat.[4] It is hard to imagine Noah and his family accomplishing this task!

The proposed answers to this question are groundless speculations, none of which the Bible justifies. Perhaps Noah had access to a more superior technology. Perhaps he employed a number of the people who would soon be destroyed by the flood. (The irony! But it corresponds to the Mesopotamian accounts.) Perhaps God gave Noah superhuman strength and engineering skills. Perhaps the fallen angels helped him. (See the 2014 Noah movie based on early Jewish legends.) None of these, or any other explanations, are likely, and the Bible suggests nothing more than that Noah and his family built the ark.

Let's remember that the ark as described in the Bible, if taken as precise measurements of an actual boat, is larger than any wooden boat built not just in antiquity but at any time, including today. And let's face it, if Ham's ark is seaworthy or not in principle (highly dubious, and, of course, it is not going to be put in the water), there has never ever been a wooden boat nearly as large as the ark.

When we look into shipbuilding throughout history, the earliest vessels, rarely more than ten feet in length, were made of skin and reeds, and generally sailed in the marshes and along riverbanks. When advancing technology moves beyond boats used for fishing, sailing vessels that could navigate in the Mediterranean began to appear. Egyptian art as early as the Old Kingdom (2500 BC) depicts ships that may be as long as 170 feet. Ugaritic and Phoenician texts in the second and first

---

[4]For the rather stretched (to be kind) explanations one has to give to rationalize the size of the ark and its logistics, and the care and feeding of such a large group of animals by eight people, see John Woodmorappe, *Noah's Ark: A Feasibility Study* (Santee, CA: Institute of Creation Research, 1996). Only the most gullible can possibly believe all of the exceptional conditions that are needed to understand the description of the flood story as anything but hyperbolic.

millennium BC are no longer than this. Even once we move into Roman times, in the first couple of centuries AD, the most famous large vessel was the Isis, which sailed between Alexandria and Rome. Remarkably it was 180 feet by 45 feet by 44 feet—less than a quarter the size of the ark.[5]

Moving to more recent times, from the mid-eighteenth century to the early twentieth century in the modern era, a handful of 300-plus foot wooden boats have been built. The USS *Dunderberg* is often listed at the longest at 377 feet, but 50 feet of the length is a ram, so to compare to the ark we should list it at 327. The *Wyoming*, also built in the nineteenth century, is listed at 449 feet, but this includes the jib boom; actually it is 329 feet. These modern long wooden boats are also built with iron bolts and steel supports, something not available to Noah.[6] Even so, these modern wooden boats were notoriously unstable in the water.

Again, we raise these issues not to deny the Bible but to try to understand the truth as the ancient reader would have understood it. The original readers would have realized that we are dealing with a figurative description of the flood as intended by the author of the story. This is supported by the fact that it is characteristic of flood accounts in the ANE that the size and shape of the boat are hyperbolic and inherently not seaworthy (see proposition eight).

And then the flood itself is described in what to ancient readers would have been seen as hyperbolic language. The waters come from "the springs of the great deep" and flow from "the floodgates of the heavens" (Gen 7:11), reflecting an ancient cosmology where under the flat earth were the subterranean waters and above the firmament were waters (note the blue sky) that could be released by opening the gates of heaven.

---

[5]For extensive treatment, see Lionel Casson, *Ships and Seamanship in the Ancient World* (Baltimore: Johns Hopkins University Press, 1995).

[6]In the earliest times, sewn boats were standard, in which ropes were passed through holes in the planks to pull them together. Reeds were also important construction materials.

As the waters flowed from deep within the earth and from the sky, "they lifted the ark high above the earth" (Gen 7:17). Even the "high mountains" were covered (Gen 7:19), and not just covered but with water rising to more than fifteen cubits (twenty-three feet) above the mountains. The description truly is that of a worldwide flood, not a local flood. Though some modern readers don't see it, the original audience would have understood that such a description is hyperbole.

Genesis Depicts the Flood as a Global Event

We have come to the conclusion that in Genesis 1–11 the author intends to base his theological presentation of primordial eras on real events. We have also concluded that the author rhetorically shapes the presentation of these events. We now turn specifically to Genesis 6–9 and the account of the flood, and our first step is to acknowledge that the rhetoric applied by the author presents the flood as a worldwide, not a local, phenomenon.

Some scholars, who feel the force of the lack of any geological evidence for a worldwide flood (see proposition fifteen), want to argue that the flood was a local event and that the biblical text describes the flood as such. This line of interpretation has much in its favor, taking the biblical text seriously as well as the scientific evidence (or lack thereof).

Advocates of the local flood theory argue that the word 'erets, typically translated "earth," should rather be rendered "land." This decision leads to translations in which land replaces earth wherever 'erets appears:

> The LORD saw how great the wickedness of the human race had become on the ~~earth~~ land, and that every inclination of the thoughts of the human heart was only evil all the time. The LORD

regretted that he had made human beings on the ~~earth~~ land, and his heart was deeply troubled. So the LORD said, "I will wipe from the face of the earth [*adamah*] the human race I have created—and with them the animals, the birds and the creatures that move along the ground—for I regret that I have made them." (Gen 6:5-7)

"I am going to bring floodwaters on the ~~earth~~ land to destroy all life under the heavens, every creature that has the breath of life in it. Everything on ~~earth~~ the land will perish." (Gen 6:17)

"Seven days from now I will send rain on the ~~earth~~ land for forty days and forty nights, and I will wipe from the face of the ~~earth~~ land every living creature I have made." (Gen 7:4)

Noah was six hundred years old when the floodwaters came on the ~~earth~~ land. (Gen 7:6)

And after the seven days the floodwaters came on the ~~earth~~ land. (Gen 7:10)

And rain fell on the ~~earth~~ land forty days and forty nights. (Gen 7:12)

For forty days the flood kept coming on the ~~earth~~ land, and as the waters increased they lifted the ark high above the ~~earth~~ land. The waters rose and increased greatly on the ~~earth~~ land, and the ark floated on the surface of the water. They rose greatly on the ~~earth~~ land, and all the high mountains under the entire heavens were covered. The waters rose and covered the mountains to a depth of more than fifteen cubits.[1] Every living thing that moved on land perished—birds, livestock, wild animals, all the creatures

---

[1]Or, and this variation serves the interests of the local flood theory, this could be translated "rose more than fifteen cubits, and the mountains were covered" (NIV note). However, waters that rose only twenty-three feet would not cover any mountain.

that swarm over the ~~earth~~ land, and all mankind. Everything on dry land that had the breath of life in its nostrils died. Every living thing on the face of the ~~earth~~ land was wiped out; people and animals and the creatures that move along the ground and the birds were wiped from the ~~earth~~ land. Only Noah was left, and those with him in the ark. The waters flooded the ~~earth~~ land for a hundred and fifty days. (Gen 7:17-24)

But God remembered Noah and all the wild animals and the livestock that were with him in the ark, and he sent a wind over the ~~earth~~ land, and the waters receded. (Gen 8:1)

The waters receded steadily from the ~~earth~~ land. (Gen 8:3)

And [Noah] sent out a raven, and it kept flying back and forth until the water had dried up from the ~~earth~~ land. (Gen 8:7)

But the dove could find nowhere to perch because there was water over all the surface of the ~~earth~~ land (Gen 8:9)

Then Noah knew that the water had receded from the ~~earth~~ land. (Gen 8:11)

By the twenty-seventh day of the second month the ~~earth~~ land was completely dry. (Gen 8:14)

"Bring out every kind of living creature that is with you—the birds, the animals, and all the creatures that move along the ground—so they can multiply on the ~~earth~~ land and be fruitful and increase in number on it." (Gen 8:17)

Let us begin by saying that the local flood interpretation is a noble attempt at holding fast to the Bible and also making sense of the telling lack of scientific evidence for a global flood.[2] On the surface, it may

---

[2]We use *global* here in the sense of worldwide. The ancient human author and his original audience would not have known that the earth was a globe. While *global* thus is an

even appear to be convincing. However, in the final analysis, we and many others remain unconvinced. Other details of the description of the flood in Genesis seem hard, even impossible, to reconcile with the idea that in Genesis 6–8 we have the depiction of a local flood, one of only partial coverage, even one of gargantuan proportions.

For instance, the emphasis at the beginning of the story is on the pervasiveness of human sin, which leads God to regret the creation of human beings (Gen 6:11-13) at large, not just those in a circumscribed place. Can we imagine all human beings at this time were in one specific place that could be covered by a large, local flood? Of course, it is difficult to answer this question because the Bible does not tell us when the flood took place. Nor does it provide information about the distribution of humans from the moment of their creation. For that matter, the location of Noah's family isn't named either.[3] This information is not necessary for the story because the picture described in Genesis 6–8 is not a local flood but one that covered all the earth and destroyed every human and animal except those on board the ark. In any case, we should also note that the emphasis since Genesis 4 at least has been on the dispersal of human beings.[4] The impact and significance of the flood is universal, but again, that does not mean that its geographical scope is.

The biblical text itself is enough to undermine the idea that the text describes a local flood, but science provides yet another important consideration. From what we know through scientific inquiry, humanity's history began in Africa and eventually spread to the Middle East and Europe and beyond. Thus, unless we are talking about an early

---

anachronism, we use it because it has entered the modern debate. Even so, we will use *worldwide* more often.

[3]The only geographical reference in the story is to the mountains of Ararat (Gen 8:4). While not a specific reference to a particular mountain, the region is found in eastern Turkey near Lake Van.

[4]Note Genesis 4:12 and God's pronouncement that Cain would be "a restless wanderer on the earth" (in the land?).

local flood in Africa (which would make little sense of the Ararat landing), there was no time when all humans were concentrated in a specific area so that even an extensive, regional flood could wipe them all out.

And we need to emphasize that this story describes the destruction of all humanity, save Noah and his family. The flood is a reversal of creation, which began by God creating the world in a nonordered state (*tohu wabohu*, "formless and empty" [Gen 1:2]). We can picture this *tohu wabohu* stage as a watery blob. The creation days of Genesis 1 picture the movement from nonorder to order, but God restores order after first returning the world to its precreation watery state (nonorder). God is doing a do-over. Though his act by his own admission does not eliminate disorder (= human sin [Gen 8:21]), it demonstrates his commitment to continue his order-bringing plan (Gen 8:22).

Further, if we have in Genesis 6–9 the description of a local flood, why take pairs of every kind of animal, including birds? Even if humans did not live outside the bounds of the local flood, certainly most of the animals did. Indeed, the fact that the birds needed to be included in the ark indicates that the flood waters must have risen very high indeed.

For that matter, if the flood were local, why build such a huge boat? Why not simply tell Noah and his family to move?

The reason why is because "all the springs of the great deep burst forth, and the floodgates of the heavens were opened" (Gen 7:11), not just those in a local area.

And then there is the description of the depth of the flood waters. The most natural reading of the Hebrew of Genesis 7:20 is that given in the NIV: "The waters rose and covered the mountains to a depth of more than fifteen cubits [twenty-three feet]." Let's also remember that these are no small mountains. After the waters receded, "the ark came to rest on the mountains of Ararat." In spite of the popular identification of Mount Ararat, the Bible refers only to a general region in eastern Turkey near Lake Van. But no matter which specific peak we are talking about among the mountains of Ararat, to describe the flood waters as reaching twenty-three feet over them means the biblical text does not describe a local flood. Instead, it is using intentionally universalistic language rhetorically to talk about the significance of the flood event.

In spite of its good intentions and proper motivations, the attempt to interpret the biblical text as knowingly describing a local flood remains unconvincing. But before leaving the subject, we should address another strategy for understanding the biblical text as presenting a picture of a local flood.

A variant on this view says that the flood was local, not worldwide. But from the perspective of the ancient participants (Noah and his family), the waters covered the whole earth (as far as they knew). In other words, from the participants, who are also the initial reporters of the event, this local flood did cover all the earth. The story then was presumably passed down orally or perhaps even in written form at a certain stage to come to Moses, whom advocates of this view typically see as the author, who included it in what we know today as the book of Genesis. With this view, there is no need to translate 'erets as "land," since as far as the initial reporter was concerned the (actually) local flood did cover the world.

Again, we commend many elements of this approach. Most notably it honors the principle that biblical texts (and in this case an earlier source, the *toledot* of Noah [Gen 6:9–9:28], included in a biblical text) are written from the author's "cognitive environment."[5] The Bible was written for us, but not to us. We have no reason to believe that God gave ancient authors special knowledge of perspectives on geology, cosmology, astronomy, or any other scientific information beyond that known at the time. Nor do we have any reason to think that God

---

[5]See proposition one.

embedded such information in the human author's writings beyond the latter's conscious knowledge.[6]

Though commendable for many reasons, this variant of the local flood theory is similarly unpersuasive, and for the same reasons the version described earlier does not convince. The language used in the flood story does not support the idea that the flood was only a local, even if widespread, flood. And this conclusion is, in our opinion, inescapable whether the author of the account was describing it as local or the initial reporter whose account was ultimately placed in the book of Genesis thought a local flood was actually a worldwide flood.

Let's conclude this section with a summary list of the elements of the story that lead us to conclude the flood is being described in Genesis (hyperbolically) as a worldwide, not a local flood.

1. Human sin is pervasive, encompassing all humans, not just those in a local area.

2. God regretted making human beings on the earth, not just those in a local area.

3. The flood as God's judgment is the first part of re-creation. In the creation account, God moves the cosmos from nonorder to order. The first phase should be pictured as a watery blob, which over six creation days is brought into a functional order. The flood is a reversal of order to nonorder, with the ultimate goal of

---

[6]Contra the thinking of Hugh Ross and others who work in the organization known as Reasons to Believe. See, for example, Kenneth Keathley, J. B. Stump, and Joe Aguirre, eds., *Old-Earth or Evolutionary Creation?* (Downers Grove, IL: InterVarsity Press, 2017). Also, from Paul Copan et al., eds., *The Dictionary of Christianity and Science* (Grand Rapids: Zondervan, 2017): "Reasons to Believe," 565; "Hugh Ross," 577-78; "Concordism," 104-5. Our view on this does not preclude a discussion of whether the Old Testament prophets "spoke better than they knew" concerning the central message of the Bible—namely, redemption. Evangelical Protestant scholars disagree over whether there is a *sensus plenior* (deeper meaning) when it comes to the theological message of the Bible. We have no reason to think that the Bible has a scientific *sensus plenior*, because the Bible does not show any interest in teaching about scientific subjects such as cosmology.

reestablishing order. In this scenario the flood would need to be worldwide.

4. The need to take pairs (and in some cases seven pairs) of animals, including birds, on board indicates a worldwide flood, not just a local flood.

5. The size of the boat indicates flood waters beyond the imagination of a local flood.

6. That "all the springs of the great deep burst forth, and the floodgates of the heavens were opened" (Gen 7:11) indicates a worldwide flood.

7. The height of the waters as fifteen cubits (twenty-three feet) over the mountains (Gen 7:20), and the only mountains mentioned being the sizeable "mountains of Ararat" (Gen 8:4), point to a global flood.

Thus, it is our conclusion that Genesis 6–8 describes a worldwide, not a local flood. This conclusion leaves us with what at first read, at least from our twenty-first-century Western perspective, is an error or at least a contradiction. The Bible describes a worldwide flood, yet absolutely no geological evidence supports a worldwide flood. While some people believe that this means that science must be wrong if the Bible is right, we believe that if science is right, then it leads us to a better interpretation of the biblical material, the interpretation that gets us to the original intent of the biblical author.

We have attempted to support the idea that the rhetoric related to the flood is intentionally universal but that it is actually the impact and significance that is universal rather than the range and scope. As a final example of this distinction, we offer the example of the Holocaust. People today might talk about the Holocaust in terms of the "total annihilation of European Jewry," assuming the event in its traditional and rhetorically expressed terms. The speaker describes the event in intentionally universalistic terms yet at the same time recognizes the hyperbole, as those hearing the description also would. In the end the succeeding discussion would focus not on the actual numbers, scope, or the idea that not a single Jew was left in Europe. Instead, the point would be to try to answer the question why—why would God allow such a thing? The interpretation of the event is invoked by the sheer horror of it as it is expressed in rhetorical terms.

PART 2

BACKGROUND: ANCIENT NEAR EASTERN TEXTS

Ancient Mesopotamia
Also Has Stories of a Worldwide Flood

Every serious student of the Bible knows that there are other flood stories from the ancient Near East, particularly from ancient Sumer, Babylon, and Assyria.[1] What is disputed is not the existence and relevance of these ancient flood accounts but rather their significance and relationship to the biblical story.

In this proposition we begin by describing the ancient Near Eastern material available to us, and in the next we will discuss similarities and differences between these and the biblical account of the flood.

In Sumerian, we have reference to the flood in a text commonly referred to as the "Eridu Genesis," due to its combination of a creation story as well as a flood account. After an account of the creation of humans, the emergence of the first cities, and the institution of kingship, we then get an account of the flood. The story begins with the god Enki (also known as Ea) warning his devotee, Ziusudra, the king of Shuruppak, of a coming flood commissioned by the gods Anu and Enlil. Then follows a broken part that scholars commonly think

---

[1]One brief account from Ugarit, but interestingly, none from Egypt.

contained Enki's counsel to build an ark. When the text becomes clear again, we get a brief account of the flood:

> All the evil winds, all stormy winds gathered into one and with them, then, the Flood was sweeping over [the cities of] the half-bushel baskets for seven days and seven nights. After the flood had swept over the country, after the evil wind had tossed the big boat about on the great waters, the sun came out spreading light over heaven and earth.[2]

After the waters recede, Ziusudra then offers sacrifices to the gods, who then "were granting him life like a god's, were making lasting breath of life, like a god's, descend into him." We will see that the major elements of this story are repeated in later Babylonian as well as the biblical version of the story.

The flood also receives mention in the Sumerian King List, a text that describes kingship as a gift from heaven to the first city, Eridu, and then how kingship passed from city to city. Of interest to us is that the Sumerian King List splits its accounting of kingship into a preflood period and a postflood period. The flood, thus, is simply mentioned rather than presented as a story: "There are five cities, eight kings ruled them for 241,000 years. [Then] the Flood swept over [the earth]. After the Flood had swept over [the earth] . . ."[3]

Turning to Akkadian versions of the flood story, we begin with a summary of the plot of a Babylonian epic known as Atrahasis, named after its main protagonist, who is a flood hero comparable to Noah in the biblical account. The Epic of Atrahasis is especially interesting because, like Genesis 1–11, it combines an account of the creation of human beings with an account of the flood.

---

[2]Translations of the Eridu Genesis come from Thorkild Jacobsen, *COS* 1:513-15. He is translating the oldest copy of the composition that we have dating to approximately 1600 BC.

[3]Translation from Thorkild Jacobsen in *ANET*, 265.

Since our interest is in the story of the flood, we will pass quickly over the story of the creation of humanity.[4] Humans were created when the lesser gods (the Igigi) revolted against the forced labor that the more powerful gods imposed on them (the Anunna gods). Eventually, the Anunna gods relented and replaced the Igigi in their onerous task of digging irrigation ditches by creating humans. They created humans from the clay of the earth, the blood of a minor god, and the spit of the gods.

Time passes after the creation of humanity, and their population grows. The resultant "noise" (see proposition eight) disturbs the great gods, particularly the god Enlil. After trying other means to reduce the population, Enlil then decides to wipe out humanity by means of a flood. One god, Enki (also known as Ea), disagrees with this course of action and takes steps to prevent the complete eradication of humanity.

Enlil had made the gods swear not to tell humanity of the coming disaster, but Enki gets around this prohibition by speaking not directly to Atrahasis but rather to his house (knowing that he will hear):

Wall, listen to me!
Reed wall, pay attention to all my words!
Flee the house, build a boat,
Forsake possessions, and save life.
The boat which you build,
[ ] be equal [ ]
Roof her over like the depth,
So that the sun will not see inside her,
Let her be roofed over fore and aft.[5]

---

[4]For those who are interested in this part of Atrahasis and its relationship to the biblical account, see Tremper Longman III, *Genesis*, SGBC (Grand Rapids: Zondervan, 2016), 46-51.
[5]Translations from Atrahasis are by B. Foster, in *COS* 1:450-52. For important studies on Atrahasis, see W. G. Lambert and A. R. Millard, *Atra-Hasis: The Babylonian Story of the Flood* (Oxford: Clarendon Press, 1969). See also A. R. Millard, "A New Babylonian 'Genesis' Story," *TynBul* 18 (1967): 3-18.

After he built the ark and placed animals and his family onboard, the torrential rains began:

Adad [the storm god] was roaring in the clouds.
The winds were furious as he set forth,
He cut the mooring rope and released the boat.
. . . . .
Anzu [the divine storm bird] rent the sky with his talons,
. . . .
And broke its clamor [like a pot]
[ ] the flood [came forth]
Its power came upon the peoples [like a battle].
. . . .
The deluge bellowed like a bull,
The wind [resound]ed like a screaming eagle.
The darkness [was dense], the sun was gone.

Due to damage to the cuneiform tablet, the text becomes fragmentary after this. In a reference to "like flies," we probably have a reference to the gods' reaction to Atrahasis's sacrifice after the flood, as we see in the Gilgamesh Epic's version of the flood, to which we now turn.

Perhaps the best-known Babylonian version of the flood is found in the eleventh tablet of the Gilgamesh Epic. The Gilgamesh Epic tells the story of a mid-third millennium BC king of the city of Uruk, who gives his name to the epic. At the beginning of the story, Gilgamesh is a young, impetuous ruler. He is not really evil, but he is immature in a way that harms his subjects, so much so that they pray to the gods to help them with their king.

The gods respond by creating Enkidu, a wild man of the steppe who runs with the wild animals. To bring him into the city to confront Gilgamesh, the people of Uruk send a prostitute out to him, who sleeps with him. Afterward the animals will not have anything to do with him, and he goes with her into the city. He hears about Gilgamesh and grows angry, particularly at the fact that he sleeps with all the brides of the city on their wedding night (the "right of the first night" referred to in proposition twelve regarding the "sons of God").

Thus, when Enkidu encounters Gilgamesh, they wrestle. Enkidu puts up a good fight, but in the end is defeated by Gilgamesh. At first it is not clear how the gods intended to answer the people's prayer, but after the fight Enkidu and Gilgamesh become fast friends and set out on adventures together, thus relieving the citizens of their rather boorish young king.

In the midst of their adventures, Ishtar, the goddess of love and war, sees Gilgamesh washing the blood from his naked body, and she proposes a relationship with him. He responds with insults with reference to her previous unseemly relationships that ended badly for those she slept with.

Insulted, Ishtar goes to her father Anu, the god of heaven, and asks for vengeance. He responds by sending the bull of heaven against Gilgamesh, but Gilgamesh kills the bull, rips off its forelock and throws it into Ishtar's face.

At this point, Anu kills Enkidu. As Enkidu dies in Gilgamesh's arms, the king realizes that he too will eventually die, so he sets out to do something about it. And this is what finally brings him to the flood hero, whose name in this epic is Uta-napishti. After all, Uta-napishti is the only human to have eternal life, so Gilgamesh wants to know his secret. Gilgamesh's question leads Uta-napishti to tell him the story of the flood.

As in Atrahasis, we learn that Enlil and the gods determined to destroy humanity because of their noise. We also learn that Ea, who had promised to keep the secret from humanity, told Uta-napishti's house to "destroy this house, build a ship, forsake possessions, seek life, build an ark and save life. Take aboard ship seed of all living things."[6]

---

[6]Translations from the Gilgamesh Epic come from B. R. Foster, *COS* 1:458-60.

Uta-napishti thus sets about building an ark, whose floor space was "one full acre" and had an unusual shape: "The ship which you shall build, let her dimensions be measured off. Let her width and length be equal."[7] After its construction, he gathered silver, gold, his family and relatives, the skilled craftsmen who built the ark, plus "beasts of the steppe, wild animals of the steppe."[8]

Then the gods sent the storm and tore down the dikes so that the flood was "passing over the people like a battle." The flood was so fearsome that even "the gods became frightened of the deluge, they shrank back and went up to Anu's highest heaven." In what follows, Uta-napishti gives a rather uncomplimentary picture of the gods' re-action: "The gods cowered like dogs, crouching outside, Ishtar screamed like a woman in childbirth." Indeed, Belet-ili, the goddess of the womb and the one described as the creator of humanity, bemoans her agreement to Enlil's plan for destroying humanity.

Eventually the storm ended and the waters receded. The ark came to rest on Mount Nimush (also called Nisir), and after seven days, in what is perhaps the most remarkable similarity to the biblical account of the flood, he released three birds: a dove, which found no perch and so returned; a swallow, which likewise could find no perch; and a raven, which saw the waters receding, ate, and did not return.[9]

Thus, Uta-napishti and the ark's occupants exited the ark, and the flood hero's first action was to offer a sacrifice. Again, the gods' re-sponse to the sacrifice strikes us as uncomplimentary: "The gods smelled the savor, the gods smelled the sweet savor, the gods crowded around the sacrificer like flies."[10] After all, the gods depended on human offerings for sustenance.

---

[7] Some have concluded that the boat is cubical; others have postulated a ziggurat-shape. In a recently discovered tablet, the boat is circular, making length and width equivalent of the diameter.

[8] In the Eridu Genesis, the animals were the "small animals" (line 182, COS 1:515).

[9] Tablet 11:148-56.

[10] B. R. Foster, COS 1:460.

Once he realized that some humans survived the deluge, Enlil grows angry, particularly with Ea. Ea responds to Enlil's anger by challenging him: "You, O warrior, are the sage of the gods, How could you, unreasoning, have brought on the deluge?"[11] He goes on to counsel Enlil to handle the problem of overpopulation with less extreme measures by using predator animals, pestilence, or famine.

By describing the flood, Uta-napishti answers Gilgamesh's question about how he and his wife acquired the status of immortality: "Enlil came up into the ship. . . . He touched our brows, stood between us and blessed us, 'Hitherto Utnapishtim has been a human being, now Uta-napishti and his wife shall become like the gods.'"

By recounting the story of the flood to Gilgamesh, Uta-napishti is telling him that the immortality he and his wife enjoy is the result of a unique circumstance. He gives Gilgamesh some hope that he might gain life by telling him about a plant at the bottom of the sea. However, after getting the plant, a serpent carried it off.

Gilgamesh, now knowing that eternal life is not accessible to him, returns to Uruk. The epic ends as Gilgamesh sees this magnificent city and marvels in it.[12] In this, we may detect a matured king returning to his city and knowing that his "afterlife" will be in terms of his reputation as a king. Thus, the hopes of the people of Uruk at the beginning of the epic are realized.

One further source warrants mention. In 2014 a cuneiform tablet about the size of a cell phone came into the possession of the British Museum. It is part of an account of the flood that features Atrahasis as the hero. The reverse side preserves only some partial lines, but the front side contains a detailed description of the construction of the ark.

In this account the ark is described as coracle-like, specified in the text as a round vessel with a diameter of about 230 feet and 20-foot-high

---

[11]Ibid.

[12]There is a wide consensus among scholars that tablet 12 does not continue the story of the first eleven tablets.

walls. As in the other accounts from Mesopotamia, this vessel is inherently not seaworthy. This boat is like a giant rope basket, using thirty wooden ribs around the circumference. It is coated with bitumen inside and out. Another intriguing detail provided only by this tablet is that the animals enter two-by-two.[13]

The text begins with Enki addressing the reed wall, as in the other accounts. Again, Atrahasis is instructed to dismantle his house to build the boat. This brief text provides an important addition to our sources for understanding the Mesopotamian traditions.

In this proposition, we have described the leading ANE sources of flood tradition outside the Bible. We have seen that the flood played a significant role in the literature of the Sumerians as well as the Babylonians and Assyrians. We next turn to an assessment of how the Mesopotamian tradition relates to the biblical story.

---

[13]This note is on the reverse of the tablet, which is only partially readable, but this word ("two-by-two") was clear enough to the translator. A translation of the tablet can be found at "Noah's Round Ark Takes to the Water," *The History Blog*, August 23, 2015, www.thehistoryblog.com/archives/38087.

Proposition 8

The Biblical Flood Account Shares Similarities and Differences with Ancient Near Eastern Flood Accounts

Now that we have described the relevant flood traditions from ancient Mesopotamia, we will describe similarities and note the differences they have with the biblical account. We will then assess the significance of these similarities and differences.

The general contours of the flood story as we hear it in the Eridu Genesis, Atrahasis, and the Gilgamesh Epic are very similar. Due to displeasure with humans, the divine realm decides to bring a flood against them to destroy them. In each case, the divine realm chooses one individual (Ziusudra, Atrahasis, Uta-napishti, Noah) to save by warning them of the coming flood and instructing them to build an ark. While the shape of the arks in the various stories differs, remarkably the floor space of the arks is nearly identical.[1] After building the ark, the flood hero and others (family and in some cases even more people) as well as animals enter the ark. The flood waters rise and

---

[1] As pointed out by Irving Finkel, *The Ark Before Noah* (New York: Nan A. Talese, 2014), 313, the round boat of Atrahasis has 14,400 square cubits of floor space as does the cubical ark in Gilgamesh. Noah's ark is slightly, but only slightly, bigger (15,000 square cubits).

finally ebb to the point that the ark comes to rest. The Gilgamesh Epic and the biblical account note that the ark settles on a mountain (Nimush [Nisir] and Ararat, respectively). In these two versions we also hear that Uta-napishti and Noah let out three birds to determine whether the waters had receded to the point that they could disembark. After stepping off the ark, the flood heroes offer a sacrifice to (the) god(s).

While the similarities are striking, so are the differences. Indeed, there are so many differences in detail that we won't mention them all, but they include things like the length and duration of the flood, the size and shape of the ark, the number and identity of people that go on the ark, the name of the flood heroes, and the order of the birds sent out to determine whether the waters of the flood had yet receded.[2]

In this proposition we will now proceed to consider about a dozen points of comparison between the biblical and ANE flood accounts. This will provide the basis for assessing their relationship. As we begin, the reader should not jump to the conclusion that the identification of similarities suggests that the biblical author has borrowed information directly from the Mesopotamian accounts. Everyone in the ancient world knows there was a flood (just like everyone today knows there was a Holocaust). It is in the cultural river. The question is, what was God up to? Why did he send it? On this point, different texts may offer vastly different interpretations. Every culture will give the general tradition its own shape. The Mesopotamian accounts are drawing out of the cultural river and spinning it according to their cultural ideas and theology. The biblical authors are doing the same. We need not

---

[2]Finkel, *Ark Before Noah*, points out that within the Mesopotamian tradition the shape of the ark moves from "naturally long and narrow, high in prow and stern" (311), then evolves into a "round coracle" (clearly described in a new tablet that Finkel presents for the first time and which he calls simply "The Ark Tablet," 311). And then we have the cube-shaped boat of Gilgamesh. The Genesis ark "is an oblong, coffin-shaped vessel of wood" (313).

concern ourselves with whether the Israelite authors have access to copies of the Mesopotamian accounts.[3]

When comparing the biblical account of the flood to the Mesopotamian accounts, we will find differences at the *description* level (such as the length of the flood, the size of ark) because each account adopted a traditional description to reflect the desired rhetorical effect. But these descriptions are incidental and don't matter. What is important is the difference in the *interpretation* of the event. Here there are noticeable differences between the ANE accounts, and the biblical account has a vastly different interpretation to offer.

PORTRAYAL OF THE GODS, THEIR PRIORITIES, AND THEIR ADMINISTRATION OF THE WORLD

Particularly notable in the comparison between the biblical and ANE accounts is the dramatic difference in the depiction of the divine realm—what the gods are like as well as how they administer the cosmos.

In the Bible, there is one God, Yahweh, who orders the flood, warns Noah in order to preserve humanity in the future, brings the flood waters, causes them to recede, receives the sacrifice offered by Noah, and enters into a covenant with creation through Noah in order to assure that the world will maintain order and stability.

In the Mesopotamian stories, many gods are involved, and they do not share the same perspectives or plans, and actually act counter to each other's interests. This is seen particularly in the relationship between Enlil and Ea. Enlil orders the flood to destroy all humanity, but Ea sees the folly of his decree since the gods are dependent on humanity for their sustenance. Thus, he works to undermine Enlil's intent by warning his devotee indirectly by speaking to the wall of his

---

[3]Indication that the Gilgamesh Epic was known early in Israelite history is found in the fragment of the account dating to the end of the second millennium (the Judges period) unearthed in the excavations at Megiddo.

reed house. The other gods (Ishtar and Belet-ili) come across as hapless bystanders who have not resisted the decree but are horrified when they see it set in motion.

Indeed, all the gods come across as flawed in their motivations and actions. Ea, along with the other gods, had agreed to keep this plan a secret from humans. He engages in casuistry and subterfuge in order to warn the flood hero. The other gods are also depicted in a less than dignified way. They cower "like dogs" at the sight of the flood and gather "like flies" at the postflood sacrifice since they are starved.

Then, of course, we have the dramatic difference regarding the number of gods. Yahweh is sovereign and supreme. His decree will not be undercut or circumvented by any power since there is no power that can match his as the Creator of everything and everyone. Thus, Yahweh both decides to send the flood as well as to preserve the human race through the rescue of Noah and his family. In the Mesopotamian narrative the survival of the flood hero depended on the rather underhanded actions of Ea, who had been sworn to secrecy but devised a clever way to warn his devotee to build an ark and survive the flood. Granted, Ea's actions prevent a disaster not so much for humanity as for the gods themselves. At the end of the account it becomes clear that Enlil, though powerful, did not think through the consequences of the flood for the sustenance of the gods themselves. Lack of foresight is represented in the ANE when they don't realize they are cutting off their own food supply. They don't regret making humans; they regret having almost destroyed them. Yahweh regrets making humans, but that does not reflect a lack of foresight on his part.

Finally, we need to notice that a significant difference exists not only in what the gods were like (attributes) but in what motivated them to action (priorities) and how they administered the world. The polytheism of the ancient world is not just a matter of how many gods there are. People in the ancient world found their own identities in their community (family and clan). The individualism of our own culture would have been unimaginable to them. But if human identity was found in community in their cultural river, so divine identity was to be found in their community. The gods of the ancient world existed in community, operated as a community, and found their identity in relationship to their community. Polytheism is thus inevitable. This community is reflected in the flood accounts, and we see the community of the gods operating as any human community does: deliberation among themselves, disagreement, agendas, power plays, betrayal, blame placing, bureaucrats, and rogues. Mesopotamian gods administered by means of a divine council, and that concept is not foreign to biblical thinking (Job 1–2; 1 Kings 22; Is 6). But that similarity is somewhat superficial. The divine council in the biblical picture is not a community of peers, because Yahweh stands alone without a community of peers. In a world where divine agency is the way everything works (whether *we* designate events as natural or supernatural), in Israel there is only one divine agent.

The gods in the ANE were motivated by what can be called the "Great Symbiosis." In works such as Atrahasis and the Babylonian creation epic Enuma Elish, we learn that the gods created people because they were tired of the work involved to meet their own needs. Gods needed food, housing, clothing, and so on, but they did not want to work for it. Once people were created to serve in this way, it becomes necessary for the gods to provide for people (if there is no rain, crops cannot grow and the gods cannot be fed) and protect them (if they are being harried by invaders who steal their food or burn their crops, the gods cannot be cared for). Throughout the literature of the ancient world, we learn it is the mandate to provide for the gods that stands as the principal feature of their religious practice. Performance equals piety. Offense is failure to meet the needs of the gods. The result is codependence.

Not surprisingly, the Mesopotamian interpretation of the flood is based on the premise of this Great Symbiosis. The gods have not created people for relationship (as Yahweh had done). The gods live among the people (in temples) so that the people can meet their needs, but they don't really like people—they need people. Yahweh, in contrast, has no needs and actually desires relationship. Living among people was his plan from the beginning, and it was why he created them.[4] This is true of all humanity but is expressed most clearly in connection to Israel in passages like Leviticus 26:11-12: "I will put my dwelling place among you, and I will not abhor you. I will walk among you and be your God, and you will be my people." The Great Symbiosis is consistently refuted in the Old Testament and has no role in the interpretation of the flood. In the Mesopotamian flood account the Great Symbiosis explains the actions of the gods at every turn. For them, the operation of the Great Symbiosis is the basis for order in the world. In the interpretation offered in Genesis, disruption of order is the driving idea, but order from the biblical standpoint has nothing to do with the Great Symbiosis. We can see all of this more clearly by looking at the reason for the flood cited in the respective interpretations of the event in Genesis and Mesopotamia.

REASON FOR THE FLOOD

This is probably the most important element to evaluate. Yahweh decreed the flood to restore the cosmic order that had been disrupted by the moral depravations of humanity ("The LORD saw how great the wickedness of the human race had become on the earth, and that every inclination of the thoughts of the human heart was only evil all the time. . . . So the LORD said, 'I will wipe from the face of the earth the human race I have created'" [Gen 6:5, 7]). On the other hand, while the Eridu Genesis and Gilgamesh do not give a reason,

---

[4]It should be noted, however, that despite this, even Yahweh at times grew weary of living among people who did not treat his presence with respect (cf. Is 1; Jer 7).

according to Atrahasis, Enlil decreed the flood because "the noise of mankind [has become too intense for me], [with their uproar] I am deprived of sleep."[5] The Akkadian words translated noise are *rigmu* and *huburu*.[6]

Suggestions for understanding these terms are numerous:

- Outcry (i.e., complaints) over hard work and call for rebellion

- Hubris represented in rebellion of overreaching human limitations (Bodi)

- Continuing petitions for relief

- Impious, irreverent, insolent, or wicked behavior (cf. the "outcry [*za'aqah*] against Sodom" in Gen 18:20 and the frequent use of the noun translated "arrogance/insolence" [Heb. *hamon*] in Ezekiel)[7] (Oden)

- Violent behavior

- Inevitable increase in noise from human overpopulation (Moran)

---

[5]Translation from W. Lambert and A. Millard, *Atra-Hasis: The Babylonian Story of the Flood* (Oxford: Oxford University Press, 1969), 67.

[6]Numerous analyses have been offered in the scholarly literature; note especially the following: Bernard F. Batto, "The Sleeping God: An Ancient Near Eastern Motif of Divine Sovereignty," in *In the Beginning: Essays on Creation Motifs in the Ancient Near East and the Bible*, ed. Bernard F. Batto (Winona Lake, IN: Eisenbrauns, 2013); Daniel Bodi, *The Book of Ezekiel and the Poem of Erra*, OBO 104 (Freiburg: Vandenhoeck & Ruprecht, 1991), 129-61; Yağmur Heffron, "Revisiting 'Noise' (*rigmu*) in Atra-hasis in Light of Baby Incantations," *JNES* 73 (2014): 83-93; Jacob Klein, "A New Look at the Theological Background of the Mesopotamian and Biblical Flood Stories," in *A Common Cultural Heritage: Studies on Mesopotamia and the Biblical World in Honor of Barry L. Eichler*, ed. G. Frame, E. Leichty, Karen Sonik, J. Tigay, and S. Tinney (Bethesda, MD: CDL, 2011), 151-76; William L. Moran, "Some Considerations of Form and Interpretation in Atrahasis," in *Language, Literature, and History*, ed. F. Rochberg-Halton (New Haven, CT: American Oriental Society, 1987), 245-56; Robert A. Oden Jr., "Divine Aspirations in Atrahasis and in Genesis 1–11," *ZAW* 93 (1981): 197-216; Takayoshi Oshima, "'Let Us Sleep!' The Motif of Disturbing Resting Deities in Cuneiform Texts," in *Studia Mesopotamica*, ed. Manfried Dietrich, Kai A. Metzler, and Hans Neumann (Münster: Ugarit-Verlag, 2014), 271-89.

[7]Bodi, *Book of Ezekiel*, 161, concludes that Hebrew *sa'aqah* = Akkadian *rigmu* and Hebrew *hamon* = Akkadian *huburu*.

- Partying

- Disruption of order (Oshima, Klein)

The issue is complicated by the fact that support for any of these options can be generated from the list of meanings carried by the common Akkadian term *rigmu*.[8] For our purposes, however, we need not choose among these, because disruption of order characterizes all of them. When we compare this to the motivation given in the biblical text, the noun *hamas* (violence), especially when combined with the general term *ra'ah* (wickedness), provides a specific element of moral corruption.[9] Yet at the same time, violence can be seen generally as involving a number of behaviors that stand in contrast to a number of words that concern rest and order. Peter Machinist has drawn attention to this in the Mesopotamian epic of Erra and Ishum. Words, ideas, and behaviors on the *violence* side of the equation include anger, arousal, destruction, punishment, and noise; in the group pertaining to *rest* are appeasement, silence, weariness, and rest as well as justice and order.[10] In light of the use of these motifs that appear in contradistinction, we gain a better view of the issues framing the flood narratives.

In conclusion, all accounts suggest the situation that motivated the gods to send the flood is increasing disorder.[11] Such disruption of order will take different forms in any given culture or piece of literature since that which constitutes cosmic order and what can disrupt it vary culture to culture. The flood is understood across all accounts to be motivated

---

[8]*Huburu* is much rarer and more controversial.

[9]*Hamas* often refers to physical harm, especially murder, but can also refer more broadly to injustice and oppression when applied to a group.

[10]Peter Machinist, "Rest and Violence in the Poem of Erra," in *Studies in Literature from the Ancient Near East*, ed. J. M. Sasson (New Haven, CT: American Oriental Society, 1984), 221-26, especially 224. He lists all the Akkadian terms that are used in each of the categories. Notice also that in the biblical account the world is characterized by violence, and Noah is identified as the one who will bring rest (Gen 5:29).

[11]"Chronic disorders and crises, as a result of which the world was bound to return into a chaotic state," Klein, "New Look," 167, and "a threat to cosmic equilibrium," 172. Cf. Oshima, "Let Us Sleep!," 285.

by encroaching disorder, and sending the flood represents a strategy to restore order. Though all descriptions are general, each literary reflection provides its own perspective on what constituted the disorder.

EXTENT OF THE FLOOD

The Mesopotamian accounts are rather vague on the extent of the flood. In terms of land coverage, the only information is found in Gilgamesh once the flood has ended. When Uta-napishti opens the window he sees shores/the edge of the sea and fourteen places where landmasses were visible (11.140-41)—so not all was totally submerged. Regarding people, Atrahasis indicates that "total destruction" was called for by the gods, and in Gilgamesh, observing the aftermath of the flood, "all the people had turned to clay" (11.135).

The account in Genesis offers much more information on this count. The geographical extent of the flood is described in a variety of ways:

- "all the high mountains under the entire heavens were covered" (Gen 7:19)
- "covered the mountains to a depth of more than fifteen cubits" (Gen 7:20)
- "there was water over all the surface of the earth" (Gen 8:9)

Several factors, however, make these statements less specific than we might imagine. In keeping with the use of hyperbole, the rhetoric of universalism can be attested in numerous places in the Bible (for a few examples see Gen 41:57; Ex 9:6 [cf. Ex 9:19]; Deut 2:25). Examples in ancient literature that use universalistic language rhetorically are not difficult to find. A text known as *Sargon's Geography* states, "Sargon, King of the Universe, conquered the totality of the land under heaven."[12]

---

[12]Wayne Horowitz, *Mesopotamian Cosmic Geography* (Winona Lake, IN: Eisenbrauns, 1998), 67-95.

When we turn attention to the impact of the flood on humanity, we again find that the biblical text is more explicit than the Mesopotamian versions.

- "I will wipe from the face of the earth the human race I have created." (Gen 6:7)

- "I am going to put an end to all people. . . . I am surely going to destroy both them and the earth." (Gen 6:13)

- "I am going to bring floodwaters on the earth to destroy all life under the heavens, every creature that has the breath of life in it. Everything on earth will perish." (Gen 6:17)

- "I will wipe from the face of the earth every living creature I have made." (Gen 7:4)

- "Every living thing that moved on land perished—birds, livestock, wild animals, all the creatures that swarm over the earth, and all mankind. Everything on dry land that had the breath of life in its nostrils died. Every living thing on the face of the earth was wiped out; people and animals and the creatures that move along the ground and the birds were wiped from the earth. Only Noah was left, and those with him in the ark." (Gen 7:21-23)

- "Never again will I destroy all living creatures, as I have done." (Gen 8:21)

Most of these depend on the use of the Hebrew word translated "all," and the response would be the same as was given regarding the amount of land covered—that is, these are examples of universalistic rhetoric. The exception where "all" is not used is in Genesis 7:23, where it is turned around to say that "only Noah was left." This is a problematic translation. The Hebrew particle translated "only" is *'ak*. This is not the word that would be expected if the text wanted to single out Noah (and those with him) as alone surviving. The normal construction for that can be observed in Job 1:15-18 (4x) where the word *only* is Hebrew *raq*. Hebrew *'ak* usually begins a clause, so comparable examples of the syntactical construction in Genesis 7:23 (following a *wayyiqtol* verbal form) are difficult to identify.[13] It regularly functions either as asseverative (e.g., "surely") or adversative (e.g., "yet"). In either of those cases, however, the particle should have led the clause.

In conclusion, both Hebrew and Akkadian texts are vague about the human survivors, which is no surprise since people would have only limited knowledge of populated areas across the known world. The widespread nature of the destruction is indicated by the use of universalistic rhetoric well-known for cataclysmic events, especially of a cosmic nature, in the ancient world.

LENGTH OF THE FLOOD

The Mesopotamian accounts consistently indicate that the flood lasted seven days and nights. This is in stark contrast to the biblical account in which the rain lasts forty days and nights, but all the time periods mentioned in the Genesis text add up to one year.[14] All of these are identifiably formulaic numbers that consistently carry rhetorical value. Whether the biblical text is interested in commenting on calendrical issues, as Qumran interpreters thought,[15] the fact remains that the evidence from the ancient world and biblical usage indicates that we are not to read these time frames as specific or precise designations of actual time spans. We cannot reconstruct how long the rain lasted or the length of the aftermath of the flood from the information given. That sort of information is not given; instead, it is designed to convey the massive scope of the cataclysm.

---

[13]The only other occurrences I could find are different because the verb is a verb of speaking, in which case *'ak* still begins the clause.

[14]Technical articles argue about the ways the various numbers in the text ought to be overlapped and therefore come out with a different total, but one of the most common understandings puts the length at 365 days.

[15]4Q252; see Jeremy D. Lyon, *Qumran Interpretation of the Genesis Flood* (Eugene, OR: Pickwick, 2015), 69-94.

Identification of the Hero

The names given for the flood hero have in common that they are more epithets than names. This will be discussed in proposition eleven (see note 7). Beyond the name, the role of the character is also worth comparing. When Uta-napishti's lineage is provided, he is identified as the son of Ubar-tutu, who in turn is identified in the Sumerian King List as the last king before the flood.[16] He reigns in the city of Shuruppak. Uta-napishti is also included as one of the offspring of the Watchers in the Jewish Book of Giants.[17]

Though the royal status of the flood hero is therefore confirmed, the priestly status is asserted in the Sumerian version.[18] In other accounts the flood hero in Mesopotamia is a favorite of the god Enki, just as Noah is a favorite of Yahweh, but nothing in the description suggests that either one had a priestly position.

On a final note we should observe that not only is the text reserved regarding the information it gives about Noah, Noah himself is totally silent. Unlike characters like Abraham or Moses, he is a flat character—no personality and only characteristics cited by the narrator. He has no response to God's announcement, no questions about the ark or the animals, no plea on the behalf of anyone else, no cries for mercy, no bursts of joyful gratitude at the prospect of being saved, no grief for a world destroyed, no impatience in the ark, no prayers of thanksgiving accompanying sacrifice.[19] The text could not be clearer that Noah is a bit player and that the main role in the account is played by God.

---

[16]Andrew George, *The Babylonian Gilgamesh Epic* (Oxford: Oxford University Press, 2003), 154. This identification persists all the way through to the account of Berossus in the Hellenistic period.

[17]John C. Reeves, "Utnapishtim in the Book of Giants?," *JBL* 112 (1993): 110-15. That would include him among the Nephilim.

[18]The Eridu Genesis refers to him as a "lustration priest" (*COS* 1:514).

[19]Ellen Van Wolde, *Stories of the Beginning* (Ridgefield, CT: Morehouse, 1996), 124.

WHAT AND WHO ARE BEING SPARED

Noah is chosen because he "was a righteous man, blameless among the people of his time, and he walked faithfully with God" (Gen 6:9). Conversely, the destruction decreed by Enlil was to be total. All humanity was to die without exception. Nevertheless, the god Enki determined to save some, focusing on his favorite, Uta-napishti. In so doing, Enki is working against the decision of the divine council, but that is not the only act of treachery/trickery. In the Mesopotamian versions, the flood hero, on the advice of Enki, employs a strategy of deception in communicating to the population of Shuruppak. If it were communicated to the elders and the people that the gods were angry and going to send a flood, everyone would want to be aboard the boat. They would not adopt a posture of skepticism. Unlike the extrabiblical traditions connected to Noah in which he went out to try to persuade people to join him in the ark, Atrahasis has to give an explanation that suggests the problem is with him, not with everyone. The gods are angry with him, so he has to go away. He subsequently engages the people of the city to help prepare for his departure to the realm of Enki.

As noted in the last section, Noah is not portrayed as interacting with other people at all in the text of Genesis. The Sibylline Oracles reflect the opinion found in Second Temple literature as Noah makes an impassioned and lengthy speech condemning the people and announcing the flood.[20] In the New Testament, 2 Peter 2:5 refers to the preaching of Noah but offers no details. It is likely reflecting the intertestamental interpretation that was familiar in the first century; it is certainly not reflecting anything found in Genesis. We could imagine that, as a righteous man, Noah would have taken some sort of principled stand against the rest of the population, but we must remain focused on the interpretation the author of Genesis offers rather than to engage in elaborate speculation.

---

[20]Sibylline Oracles 1.175-233.

From our own modern cultural river, we could assume that the population would react to the announcement of an impending flood with skepticism. But in the ancient cultural river, that would not be the case. Ancient peoples would have readily accepted that the gods would wipe out everyone. They would have more likely clamored to get onboard rather than ridiculing Noah.[21] Furthermore, textual evidence argues against Noah engaging in evangelistic activity. Noah was instructed precisely who would be brought on the ark, and space was made for eight passengers. No others are anticipated or given opportunity.

When we observe the people given passage on the ark in the Mesopotamian traditions, there is a contrast compared to the eight members of a single family in Genesis. Atrahasis and the Eridu Genesis are vague or broken, but in the Gilgamesh Epic, not only the hero and his family are saved but also a variety of craftsmen.[22] This suggests that the intention was not only to spare human life but to save human culture—in fact, to preserve society and its order.

In both the biblical and Mesopotamian accounts, animals are gathered onto the ark. In Atrahasis it specifies both cattle and animals of the steppe.[23] In the Eridu Genesis, only "small animals" are included.[24] In Gilgamesh the presentation of animals is qualified by the line "whatever seed I had of living things."[25] In Genesis, categories of animals are listed numerous times (Gen 6:7, 19-20; 7:14; 8:17-19), thereby providing more detail than any of the ANE counterparts. Other comparisons are found in the designation of bringing the animals in pairs (Gen 6:19-20; 7:15; as well as the Ark Tablet) and in the specification of clean animals (Gen 7:2-3, 8;

---

[21]Note how readily the people of Nineveh in the book of Jonah accepted the credibility of Jonah's announcement of destruction.

[22]Gilgamesh 11:85-86.

[23]Atrahasis 3:2:36-37; and Gilgamesh 11.86.

[24]COS 1:515.

[25]Gilgamesh 11.84, translation by George, *Babylonian Gilgamesh Epic*, 709.

Atrahasis 3.2.32). Even though the biblical text does not draw a distinction between clean and unclean animals until the Torah, the idea that some animals were eligible to use for sacrifice and others were not is not new to the Torah. Certainly the flood traditions including this detail have anticipated that some animals were offered as sacrifices after the flood.

Finally, we learn that objects of value were also taken aboard—specifically, in Gilgamesh, silver and gold—thus indicating again that what is being saved extends beyond living things.

DESCRIPTION OF THE BOAT

Dimensions. Though the shape of the vessel differs from one account to the other, they all have in common the fact that the dimensions are impractical—none of them could have possibly been seaworthy. It would not be unusual, however, to find that the literary descriptions of dimensions in ancient Near Eastern literature would be unrealistic. A literary inclination toward hyperbole could be offered as an explanation, but other factors could likewise be identified.[26]

One such factor is that in the dimensions given we may have examples of the use of "academic arithmetic." Andrew George has proposed just such an understanding of the dimensions of the temple in Babylon, Esagila.[27] In his conclusion he states:

---

[26]See proposition five for discussion regarding wooden ships in the modern era.

[27]Andrew George, "The Tower of Babel: Archaeology, History and Cuneiform Texts," *AfO* 51 (2005): 75-95. "The use of language from academic arithmetic, the interest in the combined area of two courtyards of the neighboring temple E-sangil as material for a mathematical exercise (¶¶1-3), the presence in the same document of linear measurements based on different cubit-standards, and the presentation of the dimensions of the base of E-temen-anki as examples of how such measurements can be variously converted into area expressed in the respective capacity-surface systems, all these features indicate that the text is still more abstract and academic than an architect's plan. The suspicion must be that as an extrapolation of arithmetical and geometric problems taking as its subject idealized dimensions of Marduk's temple precinct and ziqqurrat, the text of the E-sangil Tablet originated as a compilation of training exercises in mathematics for would-be surveyors" (77).

The E-sangil Tablet, formerly understood as offering an accurate physical description of Babylon's ziqqurrat, has been characterized as a document more interested in abstract ideas than real buildings, and in consequence the question has been raised as to whether a ziqqurrat like the one described by it was ever really built.[28]

A second factor to be considered relates to a comparison with iconography in the ancient world. The depiction of human figures rarely represents the actual physical size of the individual. Conventions and rhetorical objectives were more responsible for the depiction (even when the medium would have allowed a realistic representation). A good example is found in the wall reliefs at Karnak. There the pharaoh is depicted as giant in size, far larger than any human being. In contrast, the enemies he is defeating are very small. When characters are represented smaller or larger, this is not to suggest the real size of the individual. Rather, a variety of elements determine the size represented. It is the same with a literary representation. Conventions and rhetoric determine the literary dimensions. Realism is not the objective. An unrealistic size was recognized by the audience as an acceptable convention and was not the basis for deciding whether a depiction is true or not. Truth was related to rhetoric, not to whether it was realistic.

In light of the recognition of academic arithmetic in the ancient world and the practice noted in iconography to supersize that which is important, we suggest that in the dimensions of the vessels in the various accounts, more than hyperbole is going on. That is, we are not suggesting the boat was actually only half the stated size and they doubled it to aggrandize the size of the vessel. The dimensions are not relative to the actual size. Alternatively, the dimensions can be viewed as devised with a rhetorical effect in mind. Neither jibes by skeptics about the impossibility of the vessels nor the apologetic defenses of

---

[28]Ibid., 92.

practicality and realism are to the point. Both groups are reading the text through their modern filters and thereby expect to conform to how such information would be conveyed in our current-day cultural river.

Materials. In the Mesopotamian versions, the flood hero is instructed to demolish his house (generally assumed to be the reed hut that appears elsewhere in the account) in order to build the boat. In some interpretations, the ark in these traditions recapitulates sacred space (ziggurat shaped),[29] but in others it recapitulates the typical shape of boats (round coracle). Its materials include reeds, wood, and ropes, and the whole is coated with bitumen. There is no evidence to suggest that the ark in Genesis recapitulates sacred space. The rectangular dimensions suggest instead that it recapitulates the standard shape of boats. As noted earlier, that does not mean that the dimensions are realistic (they are patently not).

The materials listed in Genesis 6:14 have presented problems for all interpreters. The vessel is called a *tebah*, which also describes the small craft that kept baby Moses afloat. The main construction material is generally understood to be a type of wood described as *gopher*, a term that occurs only here. The next term is traditionally rendered "rooms" (*qinnim* not introduced by a preposition), also occurring only here. Then the final ingredient is the bitumen to waterproof the vessel. The term used here (*kopher*) is not the normal Hebrew word for bitumen; it is borrowed from Akkadian (*kupru*).

It has recently been recognized that the second term probably does not refer to "rooms" but to "reeds." It would be odd to mention rooms here since the text does not get to the interior of the ark until later. Here the text is addressing building materials. The use of reeds as caulk between the wood (then covered with bitumen) is not only known in

---

[29]Cory Crawford, "Noah's Architecture," in *Constructions of Sacred Space IV: Further Developments in Examining Ancient Israel's Social Space*, ed. Mark K. George (New York: Bloomsbury, 2013), 1-22, esp. 14.

the ancient world but is perhaps how the building of the ark in the Babylonian accounts is described.[30] Whether reeds were used to fill the seams in the wood or for some other purpose, the use of reeds as building material is another similarity between Genesis and the Babylonian accounts. This suggests some use of reeds in the construction. This would stand as the common denominator between this vessel and that of Moses.[31]

If the second and third terms are both loanwords from Akkadian, the first term, *gopher*, also unique in Hebrew text, should also be examined as a potential loanword. In Genesis we have *gopher* covered with *kopher*. The latter, *kopher*, is a loanword from Akkadian *kupru*. We might expect, then, that *gopher* may be an Akkadian loanword from *gupru*. Intriguingly, in Akkadian, *gupru* is a reed hut.[32] Even though Noah is not told to dismantle anything, it is possible that he is constructing his boat from reed stalks, whether from his house or not. If that is the case, the verse would read: "Make for yourself a vessel of stalks from a reed hut; (with) reeds you will make the vessel and tar it inside and out with bitumen."[33] If we are correct that the biblical account uses three Akkadian loanwords in the description of the materials used to build the ark, that could add reasons to think that the biblical author is aware of Mesopotamian traditions. Against that claim, however, is that the narrative flow concerning the building materials does not specifically follow any of the Mesopotamian traditions.

---

[30]Compare Akkadian *qa-ne-e* to Hebrew cognate *qanim*. John Day, "Rooms or Reeds in Noah's Ark? *qnym* in Genesis 6:14," in *Visions of Life in Biblical Times*, ed. Claire Gottlieb, Chaim Cohen, and Mayer Gruber (Sheffield, UK: Sheffield Phoenix, 2016), 47-57. Reeds and reed workers are mentioned both in Atrahasis and Gilgamesh.

[31]There it is a different word for reeds because papyrus, one type of reed, is specified.

[32]*CAD* G 118, s.v. *gubru*. This word is used in the Gilgamesh Epic (1.37), but it is not used in the flood account in the epic, where the word for reed hut is *kikkish* (11.21).

[33]The Hebrew word for "stalks," *'ets*, can refer to trees, to planks from trees, to wooden implements made from trees, or to stalks of woody plants. Note, for example, "stalks of flax" in Josh 2:6. In the Gilgamesh Epic, one of the materials is "palm fibre" (11.54). If such is the case, the text does not refer to lumber from a *gopher* tree.

MECHANISMS OF THE FLOOD
AND THE SUPPORTING COSMIC GEOGRAPHY

As would be expected, both Genesis and the ANE accounts describe the mechanics of the storm in terms of their beliefs about both the cosmic realm and the divine realm. In Gilgamesh and Atrahasis, the storm god is bellowing and trampling the land. Weirs/dikes overflow, and the people experience lightning, blowing wind, darkness, downpour, gale, and deluge. These are all typical (if extreme) characteristics of any major storm. Nothing in the description characterizes it as a one-time event.

In the biblical account, of course, multiple gods acting from the divine realm are not mentioned. But the cosmic realm is understood in much the same way as throughout the ancient world. The description in Genesis 7:11 (cf. Gen 8:2) indicates "all the springs of the great deep burst forth, and the floodgates of the heavens were opened." The "deep" (Heb. *tehom*, cf. Gen 1:2) refers to the subterranean ocean.[34] The Apsu is not brought into the description of the flood in the ANE texts. Likewise, the ANE accounts do not address the bursting forth of the heavenly ocean (though they believed in cosmic waters situated above the solid sky). Consequently, since the cosmic mechanisms cited in the Mesopotamian texts do not include the two large bodies of water that frame the cosmos (waters above and below), we can see that the flood is not presented in the ANE versions as a cosmic event of the same magnitude as found in the description in Genesis.

---

[34]It is cognate to the Akkadian *tamti*, referring to the visible cosmic seas, but here, since the springs burst open, it must refer to what in Akkadian is called the Apsu, the subterranean cosmic seas. For detailed discussion, see Horowitz, *Mesopotamian Cosmic Geography*, 334-47. The springs that burst open are the usual places where water from subterranean sources usually surface. In the same way, the floodgates or windows of heaven describe the usual way that water from the heavenly cosmic waters enters the human realm. Consequently, the restraints are lifted on the boundaries of both cosmic oceans (waters above and waters below). There is no parallel to the terminology or the concept of the windows of heaven in ANE literature.

LANDING PLACE

The landing place for the ark in Gilgamesh is on Mount Nimush (formerly read Nisir) in the Zagros Mountains east of the Tigris.[35] In the Mesopotamian worldview the known world comprised a single continent fringed with mountains (such as the Zagros Mountains in the east and the mountains of Ararat in the north) and ringed by the cosmic sea. These mountains defined the boundaries of their knowledge of the world, and the land so circumscribed was much smaller than the way we think about continents today. The Babylonian world map from the sixth century BC shows the cosmic seas encircling a land mass that ends with Assyria and Urartu.[36]

In Genesis the landing place is in the mountains (plural, so identifying a mountain range not a single peak) of Ararat (= Urartu), some four hundred miles north of Mount Nimush, though both are in modern-day Kurdistan. It is significant to note that if the biblical account were simply adopting a Mesopotamian one, we might expect Genesis to refer to the same mountain. If someone were to suggest that the biblical author was borrowing but changed the mountain to associate the text more specifically with Israel, certainly the mountains of Ararat would make no sense. This therefore stands as an important distinction because this is not a matter of different interpretations by different cultures; this is a specific detail.

BIRDS

The employment of birds to discover whether the survivors can disembark from the ark has been considered one of the most significant evidences for the interdependence of the biblical and Mesopotamian accounts since the logic of a flood account would not inherently demand such an episode. At the same time, we note that the birds are

---

[35]Modern-day Pir Omar Gudrun. George, *Babylonian Gilgamesh Epic*, 1, 516.
[36]Horowitz, *Mesopotamian Cosmic Geography*, 321.

different. In Gilgamesh the dove is used first and returned; then a swallow, which also returned; finally, a raven was sent and was seen flying around and eating, and did not return. Too little is known about the use of birds to discover a logic that would explain their employment in such a context or the significance of differences between the traditions.

SACRIFICE

All the accounts hold in common the idea that upon disembarking from the ark the survivors offered a sacrifice to the gods. Unsurprisingly, this scene in each tradition reflects the differing deep beliefs between cultures. In Mesopotamia the fundamental belief driving the shape of the account is what we have described as the Great Symbiosis. The gods have been seven days without food, and the sacrifice provides for them, at the same time serving to appease the anger of the gods that motivated the flood. The fact that the gods need humanity is thus confirmed, and the result is that the gods need to be more circumspect in the future about taking action that is going to work against their interests. The gods, therefore, stand chastened.

In contrast, the biblical account predictably correlates with what the Israelites believed about Yahweh. He has no needs and has not become unaccountably angry such that he needs to be calmed down. The "pleasing aroma" of Genesis 8:21 functions exactly as it does within the framework of the sacrificial system in the Torah. There is no sense that Noah is interacting with a needy god who easily loses his temper.

AFTERMATH AND FATE OF THE HERO

In the Mesopotamian accounts the gods have to decide what to do with the survivors since they had not intended for any to survive. This is the point where the wisdom speech of Enki/Ea can be found (Atrahasis and Gilgamesh). Ea, the god of wisdom who had made a way for Uta-napishti to survive, chides Enlil by saying, "On him who commits a sin, inflict his crime! On him who does wrong, inflict his wrong-doing!"[37] In the interpretation of the event in Mesopotamia, we can therefore see the idea that the gods learned a lesson—they needed humanity and should be more discreet in how they deal with offense. Nothing is offered that people should learn from the event.

A sign is then given by Nintu (in Atrahasis; Belet-ili in Gilgamesh), in her role as the creator of humanity, to vouchsafe that she will never forget this debacle engineered by the gods. The sign she gives is the lapis lazuli necklace she wears. In Atrahasis she specifically refers to the "flies" being the lapis around her neck (3.6.2; cf. Gilgamesh 11.164-67). The text had previously indicated that the gods gathered like flies around the sacrifice that was offered (since they were famished from lack of food) and had also referred to flies that Anu made for Belet-ili.[38] Fly necklaces are known in the ancient world,[39] and Anne Kilmer has suggested that the iridescent wings of the flies would offer a visual reminiscent of the rainbow in Genesis.[40]

Finally, we turn our attention to the destiny of the flood survivor. In the Eridu Genesis, Ziusudra's kingship is again recognized and they grant him "life like a god's . . . making lasting breath of life, like a god's, descend into him."[41] He is then consigned the privilege of living in Mount Dilmun (modern Bahrain, considered a faraway, half-mythical place in Mesopotamian literature). In Gilgamesh, Uta-napishti and his wife are blessed by Enlil (11.202) and, instead of being counted among humankind, will now be like the gods (11.203-4) and will live faraway at the mouth of the rivers (also identified as Dilmun/Bahrain).

---

[37]George, *Babylonian Gilgamesh Epic*, 715 (11.185-86).

[38]See extensive discussion in W. G. Lambert and A. R. Millard, *Atra-Hasis: The Babylonian Story of the Flood* (Oxford: Clarendon Press, 1969), 163-64.

[39]See discussion and photo in John Walton, "Genesis," in *The Zondervan Illustrated Bible Backgrounds Commentary: Old Testament* (Grand Rapids: Zondervan, 2009), 1:53.

[40]Anne Draffkorn Kilmer, "The Symbolism of the Flies in the Mesopotamian Flood Myth and Some Further Implications," in *Language, Literature, and History*, ed. F. Rochberg-Halton (New Haven, CT: American Oriental Society, 1987), 175-80.

[41]*COS* 1:515 (lines 180-81).

When we compare this information to Genesis, an intriguing array of associations can be identified. The sign in Mesopotamia is for the gods to remember, as it is for God to remember in Genesis 9:15-16, so it serves a similar purpose whether the flies and the rainbow can be associated or not.[42] The main difference is that in Mesopotamia it serves as a reminder of the past, while in Genesis it is connected to a covenant that concerns how God will work in the future. Again we have a case in which a similar element is present in the narrative but is interpreted in different ways in the respective traditions.

In place of the wisdom saying of Ea, Genesis features the covenant as the climax of the account. Unlike the wisdom message of the Gilgamesh Epic that offers a principle by which the gods should operate, in Genesis the wisdom message comes in terms of a commitment (Gen 8:21) rather than a correction, followed by a wisdom saying about the stability of order (Gen 8:22). Yet in the covenant with humanity, accountability is also discussed (Gen 9:5-6). It is not accountability for God (as had been suggested in Ea's speech) but accountability for humans (and even animals). As before, similar story elements but interpreted very differently. Nevertheless, there is nothing in the Mesopotamian accounts to correlate with the covenant in Genesis.

Finally, when we compare the new destiny of the survivor in Mesopotamia to what we find in Genesis, Adam, not Noah, comes to mind. It is with Adam that God comments that humans have become like the gods (Gen 3:22), and it is Adam who is taken (Gen 2:15) and relocated in sacred space.[43] So Uta-napishti's destiny can be compared to Adam's when Adam is relocated in the garden and given access to the tree of life. But Adam's becoming like the gods is the consequence of eating from the tree of wisdom and results in losing precisely that which Uta-napishti is given. The same issues are under discussion, but

---

[42]Interestingly, it is not designed as a sign for people but for God.
[43]The Hebrew verb here is cognate to the Akkadian verb that indicates Uta-napishti is taken and relocated (11.206).

the interpretation and perspectives of Genesis vary notably from what we find in the ANE literature.

Historical Context

Where in history would a Babylonian locate the flood? Obviously well before Gilgamesh (a king of Uruk in the Early Dynastic period, mid-third millennium BC). Several of Gilgamesh's predecessors (e.g., Enmerkar, Lugalbanda) are known from epic literature and occur in the Sumerian King List as kings after the flood. No royal inscriptions date to before the Early Dynastic period (beginning in 2900),[44] because writing prior to that time was still in a fledgling form (emerged about 3200 BC). According to Jacobsen's interpretation of the list and the resulting calculations, seven kings spanned the time period between the flood and Enmerkar. If accurate (and much is uncertain), this would locate the flood in the latter part of the fourth millennium at the earliest.

In the biblical record, eight generations are listed between Shem and Abram. Though it is recognized that we cannot use genealogies or king lists to "just do the math" (see proposition ten), we still recognize that the information we have points us to the second half of the fourth millennium. This is the roughest of estimates and is used here only to indicate that all of these traditions target roughly the same time period.

Literary Use and Purpose

As we examine the flood accounts with regard to their literary purpose, we find a good deal of continuity. Though the biblical account interprets the flood differently, it shares with the ANE accounts the idea that the flood was represented as the setting up of a new order: out with the old, in with the new. The gods use such forces to restore order when they perceive it has deteriorated. In both the Bible and the ANE,

---

[44]Douglas Frayne, *Presargonic Period (2700–2350)*, RIME 1 (Toronto: University of Toronto, 2008) has the compilation of the earliest royal inscriptions.

the flood is an "order reset." These accounts use nonorder (the cosmic waters) to eliminate disorder (noise, violence) to then reestablish order.

CONCLUSION

In conclusion, we believe it is better to explain the similarities and differences between the biblical and Mesopotamian flood traditions not in terms of borrowing but rather in terms of Mesopotamia and Israel floating in the same cultural river.[45]

We believe the story goes way back to a period well before the invention of writing and, therefore, the advent of literature. In the far distant past (though we are unable to date it now) a devastating flood killed many people (see proposition fourteen). For reasons described in other parts of this book, we do not believe the flood was worldwide, but we do believe it was particularly devastating. We don't think it is possible to date the event, locate the event, or reconstruct the event in our own terms. That is not a problem because the event itself, with which everyone in the Near East is familiar, is not what is inspired. What *is* inspired and thus the vehicle of God's revelation is the literary-theological explanation that is given by the biblical author. We are interested in how the compiler of Genesis used the flood and how he described what God was doing in and with the flood.

The flood happened in the far distant past, and stories about the flood were thus passed down orally for generations from those who descended from the time the flood actually occurred. The similarities in the telling of the flood story between the Eridu Genesis, Atrahasis, Gilgamesh tablet 11, and the biblical account may be explained not necessarily by literary borrowing but by the fact that this story has been passed down from generation to generation by those who float in the same cultural river. Imperative for understanding the message is the particular shape given to this shared story by Israel. Any report

---

[45]See proposition one.

of the event, after all, is culturally embedded. We should attend to the differences in how the event is interpreted—what spin is given to it. Again, the literary-theological interpretation of the event is inspired, not the event itself.

We have noted the obvious similarities and the clear differences between the Mesopotamian and biblical stories of the flood. We do believe the origin of these stories is in an actual devastating flood, and this fits with our understanding of Genesis 6–9 being theological history. This event embedded itself in the minds of the people who lived through the experience (see proposition fourteen).

This story was passed down orally and then eventually in written form through the generations, and it became a very important vehicle to deliver a significant theological message. The theological message in the Mesopotamian story is very different from the theological message of the Israelite account. We can see the distinctive nature of the latter in the differences, primarily in their respective conceptions of the divine realm, in the different stories they tell and write about the flood.

Another way to think about the similarities and differences is to acknowledge that the Israelites are embedded in an ancient Near Eastern culture and that God speaks to them there. God gives them revelation that transcends the culture, but he speaks to them within the culture. This is not a matter of imposing the ancient Near East on the Bible (the Bible is an ANE literary document); rather, it involves the acknowledgment that they are within the ancient Near East. It's our responsibility to understand the flood story within its original context, and proposition eight has sought to do that.

Sufficient similarities exist to suggest an awareness of the ANE flood traditions, but not to suggest use of literary texts from Mesopotamia. In this sense the biblical account is fully embedded in the ancient world, but not indebted to a particular literary tradition. The flood tradition known generally in Mesopotamia is known well enough so that specific words and idiosyncratic aspects have been adapted by those who preserved the biblical traditions. But *adapted* is the key term, and that would be true even if they did have access to the literary texts. The adaptations help us realize the ways the biblical account is distinct and meaningful. How the narrator *interpreted* the flood tradition stands as the authoritative message of the text. God's inspiration of the biblical text does not mean it came about without the use of literary sources;[46] Chronicles attests to the explicit use of sources—some inspired, some not. Indebtedness at some level to ANE sources would not negate the authority of the interpretation of the event, but indebtedness has to be demonstrated, and, for the flood, no Mesopotamian text has yet provided what could have been a base text for the biblical narrative.[47]

The flood account stands as a good example of misunderstanding what the text is doing when we try to read the narrative from our modern cultural river. We have to read it as an ancient text in order not to get distracted by our modern questions. Only then can we step into the narrative for what it is and put ourselves in a position to understand the authoritative teaching of the text.

---

[46]To admit the possibility of sources does not mean accepting the classical formulation of source theory common in biblical scholarship (sources such as those designated J and P). Recent work has cast significant doubt on that way of understanding the Pentateuch in general and the flood story in particular. See Joshua Berman, *Inconsistency in the Torah: Ancient Literary Convention and the Limits of Source Criticism* (Oxford: Oxford University Press, 2017), 236-68.

[47]If we want to get an idea of what it would look like for one text to borrow from another, we can compare the flood account in Gilgamesh to the one in Atrahasis—whole lines are used, whole sections repeated. That is what is needed to confirm dependence on particular literary traditions.

PART 3

TEXT: UNDERSTANDING THE BIBLICAL TEXT LITERARILY AND THEOLOGICALLY

A Local Cataclysmic Flood Is Intentionally Described as a Global Flood for Rhetorical Purposes and Theological Reasons

The previous propositions have reached the following conclusions.

First, the genre of Genesis is theological history (see propositions two and three; see further eleven and fourteen). The narrative speaks of events that actually happened in space and time. All history is selective and interpreted according to the intention of the author as the author communicates with the audience. The focus of the author of Genesis is theological in that he is interested in describing God and his relationship with his human creatures.

Second, Genesis 1–11, and specifically Genesis 6–9, is theological history in this sense, and thus is in continuity with Genesis 12–50. However, these chapters concern the deep past with a focus on God's relationship with the whole world, rather than with a single family. And they cover an incredibly long period of time, from the creation to the period just before Abraham. Accordingly, Genesis 1–11, though theological history, has a significantly different feel to it, particularly in the use of figurative language to describe the past as well as the similarities and differences it displays with other ANE literature. In other words, the events that stand behind the stories of Genesis 1–11 (creation, fall, Cain and Abel, flood, Tower of Babel) are real, but the narratives are rhetorically shaped in order to present a theological message. The events are not inspired but rather their presentation and interpretation in the biblical text are.

Third, the biblical account describes the flood rhetorically as a worldwide deluge. Attempts to interpret the account as if it were describing only a local flood fail to persuade on close analysis. Those who argue for a local flood interpretation, like those who believe there was an actual worldwide flood, fail to recognize the rhetorical shaping of the story. The motivation of advocates of the local flood theory is good in that they recognize there is no evidence for a worldwide flood and believe that the solution to the problem of the apparent conflict between the Bible and geology is in a reassessment of the biblical text. Thus, they refuse to ignore the lack of evidence of a worldwide flood in the geological record but also want to defend the veracity of the biblical text. That is our motivation as well, but we take a different approach to the question we believe is more in keeping with the intention of the biblical text as well as the scientific evidence.

Fourth, we accept the vast scientific contention that the geological record shows no evidence for a worldwide flood at any point in the history of the earth (see proposition fifteen). We reject the desperate attempts of a handful of outlier scientists to argue to the contrary. If there were a worldwide flood, its marks would have been left in the geological record, but there are none. To acknowledge this reality is not to cave in to "godless science" but rather to recognize that the study of nature, God's other book, in the words of Pope John Paul II, serves to "purify religion," in this case by refining our exegesis.[1]

---

[1]John Paul II, "To the Reverend George V. Coyne SJ, Director of the Vatican Observatory," June 1, 1988, http://w2.vatican.va/content/john-paul-ii/en/letters/1988/documents/hf_jp-ii_let_19880601_padre-coyne.html.

Fifth, we have noted the use of hyperbolic language in the presentation of the flood story. Hyperbole exaggerates in order to produce an effect or to make a point. The disorder brought by sin is pervasive; the judgment is the destruction of nearly the total population as order is reset and the flood waters rise to twenty-three feet above the mountains. The ark is bigger than any wooden boat built in human history (up to today). We will explore the message communicated by the use of this hyperbolic presentation of the flood story in the propositions that follow.

Sixth, the similarities between the biblical flood and the Mesopotamian accounts of the flood are the result of the fact that the Israelites and the Mesopotamians float in the same cultural river. The event that stimulated the emergence of these stories was in the far distant past. The differences between the biblical and Mesopotamian accounts are of prime interest to us because we are interested in the particularly literary and theological presentation of the story. Again, though God is active in events, events are not inspired; their presentation and interpretation is.

Thus, we are brought to the conclusion that Genesis 6–9 pertains to a local flood described rhetorically as a worldwide flood to make a theological point. Such a view honors both the biblical text when read in its literary and cultural context as well as the geological evidence (or lack thereof).

We now have reached the point where we can unfold the theological purpose that has led to the rhetorical shaping of the narrative. In the next propositions we will present the case for two different (though not mutually exclusive) literary-theological readings of Genesis 1–11. These will guide us as we place the flood account in the context of the rhetorical strategy of Genesis.

Traditional interpretation has viewed the flood as an act of judgment carried out by God in response to the moral degradation that had come to characterize humanity by the time of Noah. Such a view not only can be supported from analysis of the text of Genesis but also stands as the earliest known interpretation of the flood (Second Temple period) and as the interpretation given in the New Testament. It is therefore exegetically supported, theologically sound, and a logical deduction.

Another perspective, not mutually exclusive, is the suggestion that Genesis 1–11 is interested in tracking the issue of nonorder, order, and disorder. In this view, the flood account focuses more on how God is reestablishing a modicum of order in the world as he uses nonorder (the cosmic waters) to obliterate disorder (evil and violence). Of course, the flood does not totally obliterate disorder, as God acknowledges in Genesis 8:21. But it resets the ordering process, and God indicates that the established order will not again be reset by a flood (Gen 8:21). This view focuses attention on God's continuing plan to establish order (present and future oriented) beyond the act of judging sin (past oriented), though both are legitimate perspectives.

The question at hand is not to determine which of these is true. Interpreters can make headway by assessing the *theological* value of each, and important insights can be gained from each. Such theological insight can be supplemented by a *literary* approach that seeks to determine how to account for the flow of Genesis 1–11. The traditional view sees the flood alongside other episodes that show moral failure and God's response in judgment. The narratives of Adam and Eve, Cain and Abel, and Ham's indiscretion easily fit this profile. The other narratives of Genesis 1–11, the sons of God and the Tower of Babel, clearly show that God is displeased with the direction taken and administers corrective action. In both of these latter episodes, God responds to a situation with disapproval. It is less clear whether they are guilty of moral failure (recall that in the Torah *impurity* also suggests God's disapproval but is not moral failure). For our purposes it is enough to recognize the pattern across the narratives of Genesis 1–11 that humans deviate from God's will and that God responds with consequences. This perspective will be summarized in proposition ten.

The order-disorder interpretation of the rhetorical strategy can also account for all of the narrative episodes as well as the elements such as the genealogies and the Table of Nations. This perspective will be laid out in more detail in propositions eleven and twelve.

Neither view rules out the other, and we have no need to choose one or the other. The important point that we are making is that the literary-theological interpretation of the passage (whichever way we go) takes precedence over the compulsion many feel to reconstruct the event itself. We contend, instead, the interpretation of the event by the biblical author takes pride of place and demands our attention as interpreters.

Before we actually trace these two theological approaches, a word about methodology is needed. When we deal with events in the biblical text, we should use the same approach that is appropriate for understanding characters used in the biblical narratives. Even though we are dealing with real people in a real past, what the narrator does with the characters is more important than what the characters do. And what God does through the characters is most important of all. This principle posits the authority at the literary (what the narrator does) and the theological (what God is doing) levels.

When we interpret events like the flood, we should treat the event as we do with a character. What the narrator does with the flood is more important than what the flood does, and what God does through the flood is most important of all. If this is so, then we need to articulate persuasively what the narrator and God are doing through the flood. Someone who believes in a global flood would say that God is flooding the entire globe and destroying all humanity. We are presenting an alternative understanding based in the literary and rhetorical aspects of the inspired account.

Just as we cannot get behind the literary curtain to see the characters as they "really were" (no Myers-Briggs or Enneagram personality profiling possible), we likewise cannot get behind the literary curtain to reconstruct the scientific reality of the flood. Furthermore, the New Testament has only that same literary curtain to work with (plus the traditions that have developed in the interim). The New Testament writers have no independent access to the event. Their inspiration does not grant them insider information, only authoritative interpretation of the meaning of the flood event and its application. Furthermore, they may well pick up something different in their interpretation of the flood to bring out a different perspective than what Genesis is doing. In other words, New Testament authors may repurpose an Old Testament account. As interpreters, we do not have to pit such diverse interpretations against one another—we can accept them both as legitimate interpretations of the same event.

We can witness the diverse interpretations of the flood account when we examine the earliest interpretations found in the intertestamental period. When we turn attention to them, we should not be surprised that interpreters are less interested in the rhetorical shaping of the narrative provided by the narrator in Genesis. These Second Temple Jews have their own theological agendas connected to their own time. As is true of many interpreters throughout history, they are engaged in repurposing biblical narratives for a contemporary focus.[2] The main issues that we find in that literature are

- the godliness of Noah;

- the role of the Watchers;

- the connection between Eden, Lubar (where they say the ark came to rest), and the Promised Land;

---

[2]Jeremy D. Lyon, *Qumran Interpretation of the Genesis Flood* (Eugene, OR: Pickwick, 2015). He includes the Genesis Apocryphon, *Commentary on Genesis A* (4Q252), *Exhortation Based on the Flood* (4Q370), and *Paraphrase of Genesis and Exodus* (4Q422).

- chronology of the flood and the festival calendar;
- reversal and renewal of creation;
- connecting the flood with eschatological judgment; and
- focus on the implications for the present and the future.

In these documents, just as in the New Testament, we can see an interaction with 1 Enoch. In that work, the flood is interpreted primarily as an act of judgment meant to purify the earth.[3] These texts demonstrate some attention to the issues we have identified in the context of Genesis (reversal and renewal of creation), but do not limit themselves to that interpretation. God's anger and the motivation to punish sin take center stage in these Hellenistic treatments. At the same time, significantly, they are not giving much attention to reconstructing the event. They do not manifest strictly empirical interests; they assume universalism based on their understanding of the event as archetypal (i.e., an act of judgment connected to eschatological judgment). These interpretations are treating the text figuratively (a figure of future judgment, a figure of divine grace, a figure of theological and thematic relationships). The scientific scope of a literal event assessed on the basis of empirical evidence is of little interest to them.

As we turn to the New Testament, we find that the authors focus on the judgment aspect of the flood in the same way that Second Temple literature did. This judgment was so memorable that it was used in the New Testament to illustrate the type of judgment that would come to the wicked. Peter used it, for instance, in connection with the judgment he saw coming on the false teachers. About them, he says:

> But there were also false prophets among the people, just as there will be false teachers among you. They will secretly introduce destructive heresies, even denying the sovereign Lord who bought them—bringing swift destruction on themselves.

---

[3]See 1 Enoch 10:20-22; cf. 1 Pet 3:20-21.

Many will follow their depraved conduct and will bring the way
of truth into disrepute. In their greed these teachers will exploit
you with fabricated stories. Their condemnation has long been
hanging over them, and their destruction has not been sleeping.
(2 Pet 2:1-3)

The judgment coming on these false teachers is then related to the
great judgments of the Old Testament: "For if God did not spare angels
when they sinned, but sent them to hell, putting them in chains of
darkness to be held for judgment [a reference to Gen 6:1-3]; if he did
not spare the ancient world when he brought the flood on its ungodly
people" (2 Pet 2:4-5).

Thus, the flood story anticipates future judgments, as is common in
Second Temple literature. Indeed, the judgment at the time of the
flood was so dramatic that the authors of the New Testament utilized
it in anticipation of the greatest judgment of all, the one coming at the
end of history when Jesus returns for a second time:

As it was in the days of Noah, so it will be at the coming of the
Son of Man. For in the days before the flood, people were eating
and drinking, marrying and giving in marriage, up to the day
Noah entered the ark; and they knew nothing about what would
happen until the flood came and took them all away. That is how
it will be at the coming of the Son of Man. (Mt 24:37-39)

The New Testament thus adopts the flood story as an illustration of
the truth that our God is a God who judges sin. He does not tolerate
disobedience, since he understands our propensity to promote ourselves above himself does not lead to our flourishing but to our det-
riment. In this it is used as an archetypal narrative for future eschatological judgment.

Before we conclude our look at the theme of judgment in the flood
narrative, we need to address one more question. It is not unusual for

people who advocate that a straightforward reading of Genesis 6–9 insists on a historical worldwide flood to say that these New Testament references to the flood show that the New Testament authors (and Jesus himself, who is quoted in Matthew 24) believed the flood was historical and global. If *they* believed the global flood was historical, then who are we to say otherwise even if there is no scientific evidence for the flood?

But this argument is faulty. The New Testament authors (and Jesus himself) are referring to the story in Genesis 6–9, which, we have readily admitted, describes the flood in worldwide terms. We argue that the New Testament authors (and Jesus himself) were sophisticated enough to understand that (even if some modern readers are not).

From this survey of Second Temple literature and the New Testament, we have seen that it is not unusual for different authors to use an event they know well to make a variety of theological and rhetorical points. Having surveyed what the Second Temple literature does with the flood account, we need to turn our attention to the interpretive task of determining what the compiler of Genesis is doing in Genesis 1–11 in general and with the flood in particular.

The Flood Account Is Part of a Sequence of Sin and Judgment Serving as Backstory for the Covenant

Our view has been laid out: a real flood of universal impact was the impetus for the story found in Genesis 6–9, which depicts this flood, using hyperbole, as a worldwide event for theological reasons. Since the interpretation of the event given in Genesis is what carries authority, we must understand how the biblical narrator has shaped Genesis 1–11. When we attend to the literary presentation, we note that the flood story has the same structure and follows the same literary pattern as the account of the first sin in Genesis 3. Both stories describe sin that is met by divine judgment and grace. We will briefly describe the unfolding of this pattern.

Before we move to that analysis, an important caveat must be noted. Even as we present the flood of Genesis as bringing about judgment, we want to issue a strong caution that such an interpretation does not give us a precedent interpreting any other flood (or other such calamities), ancient or modern, as the result of divine judgment. Our ability to identify a catastrophe as divine judgment depends entirely on the presence of an authoritative voice to so interpret that catastrophe. The Bible provides that authoritative interpretation for the Genesis flood; we have no such authoritative voice to interpret other events for us. Not all catastrophes are manifestations of God's anger or judgment.

Genesis 1–3

Genesis opens with an account of creation (chaps. 1–2). God creates the cosmos and all life, including human life. At the beginning of the story, men and women are morally innocent and living in a blessed condition. The latter means that they have a harmonious relationship with God, with each other, and with creation itself.

Genesis 3 then describes the first human sin. Adam and Eve reject God's commandment and insist on deciding for themselves what is right and wrong. Because of their rebellion, disorder and sin enter human experience and death becomes inevitable (as Paul will later point out in Romans 5:12-21). God judges his human creatures for their sin. Because of their sin, however, they no longer live in a blessed condition.

While the reader might expect the story to move directly from the sin to the execution of the judgment, it does not. In what we will see become a recurrent pattern, we next hear of what we might call a token of grace. "The Lord God made garments of skin for Adam and his wife and clothed them" (Gen 3:21). The gesture seems simple enough, but in actuality it is quite profound. The provision of clothes shows God's continuing concern for his sinful creatures. He helps them where they now feel vulnerable, even though their vulnerability is the result of their own rebellious act.

But the story does not end with the mention of the token of grace. It then moves on and concludes by narrating the execution of the judgment. The chapter ends by telling the reader that God forced Adam and Eve out of the garden. They no longer live in a blessed condition but must now struggle with hostility, relational dysfunction, difficult work, and even death.

The stories in Genesis 4–11 follow the same general pattern seen in Genesis 3. They are accounts of human sin, followed by a judgment speech and ending with a description of judgment. Between the divine judgment speech and the execution of judgment stands a token of God's grace.

Cain kills his brother Abel (Gen 4:8); God announces his judgment (Gen 4:11-12) and executes it (Gen 4:16); but before he does he shows his grace to sinful Cain by giving him a mark to preserve him from violence (Gen 4:15).

Soon, however, human sin has grown to mammoth proportions (Gen 6:5, 11-12). God decides to eradicate sinful humanity by means of a flood and announces his intention to do so (Gen 6:7, 13-21). He sends the flood (Gen 7:6-24), but he also extends his grace by allowing humanity to survive the flood by telling Noah to build an ark and bring his family and animals onboard (Gen 6:8, 18-21).

In Genesis 6:11-13, God announces his judgment as he describes their deep depravity (see also Gen 6:6-7). Later he more specifically announces that he will bring an end to all creatures, especially humanity, by means of a flood: "I am going to bring floodwaters on the earth to destroy all life under the heavens" (Gen 6:17).

As we saw with the two previous stories, the fall and the murder of Abel, God follows through with his judgment (Gen 7:6-24), but not before again extending a token of grace, a sign that he will not completely abandon his human creatures. The narrator tells us that "Noah was a righteous man, blameless among the people of his time, and he walked faithfully with God" (Gen 6:9). We then hear God's instruction to prepare for the coming flood by building a boat and gathering Noah's family as well as animals of every kind. Thus, in spite of this devastating judgment, humanity survives.

This particular judgment is so devastating that it has even been described as an act of uncreation.[1] Going back to the very opening of Genesis, we read: "In the beginning God created the heavens and the earth. Now the earth was formless and empty [*tohu wabohu*], darkness was over the surface of the deep" (1:1-2).[2] Before God brought the earth into functional order, it was "formless and empty." It is likely, if not certain, the author intends for us to think of the earth as undifferentiated water. From this formless and empty watery mass God creates a functional and livable earth. The flood, then, is a reversion to the watery mass, a *tohu wabohu* state.

The pattern we have identified also explains the abundance of intertextual allusions in Genesis 9:1-17 and Genesis 1–2 as well as Genesis 9:18-29. We observe, then, that one way of reading Genesis 1–9 is along the lines of creation—uncreation—re-creation.

The purpose of this section is to observe that the flood story fits into the pattern established by the account of the first sin and continued by the narrative concerning Cain and Abel. These are stories of sin, followed by a divine judgment speech, and the ultimate execution of judgment. However, between the judgment speech and the judgment itself, we have seen the consistent mention of a token of grace. Thus, these stories highlight three main theological points:

1. Humans are sinners.

2. God consistently judges sinners.

3. God remains gracious toward his sinful creatures.

We are now ready to turn attention to the grace evident in the flood narrative—particularly in the covenant God makes with Noah. First, Noah and his family do not deserve to survive the flood.

---

[1]David J. A. Clines, *The Theme of the Pentateuch* (Sheffield, UK: JSOT Press, 1978), 73-77.
[2]The NRSV represents another translation possibility: "The earth was a formless void and darkness covered the face of the deep." While this translation may indeed be correct, the difference with the NIV does not affect our point.

Noah does not earn his right to live because of his righteousness, and certainly the rest of his family does not.[3] But God desires to pursue order and reconciliation, and this love for his human creatures leads him not only to tell Noah to build the ark in order to survive the flood but to enter into a covenant with him after the waters recede.

As God delivers his instructions to Noah concerning the coming flood and the building of the ark, he also announces, "Everything on earth will perish. But I will establish my covenant with you" (Gen 6:17-18). And, sure enough, after disembarking the ark and offering a sacrifice to God, God says to Noah and his sons:

> I now establish my covenant with you and with your descendants after you and with every living creature that was with you— the birds, the livestock and all the wild animals, all those that came out of the ark with you—every living creature on earth. I establish my covenant with you: Never again will all life be destroyed by the waters of a flood; never again will there be a flood to destroy the earth. (Gen 9:9-11)

The term *covenant* (*berit*) appears for the first time in connection with Noah. A covenant, as the English translation rightly implies, is a formal agreement between two parties. In this covenant, God commits himself to the continuance of the world and its inhabitants. Though the words are directed to Noah and his sons, that commitment is given not only to them but to all the creation and its creatures. They don't have to live in fear that God will periodically bring the creation to an end. In spite of human sin, God says,

> Never again will I curse the ground because of humans, even though every inclination of the human heart is evil from

---

[3]Carol M. Kaminski, *Was Noah Good? Finding Favour in the Flood Narrative* (London: T&T Clark, 2014).

childhood. And never again will I destroy all living creatures, as I have done.

As long as earth endures,
seedtime and harvest,
cold and heat,
summer and winter,
day and night
will never cease. (Gen 8:21-22)

Again, this return to a functional, ordered state is an act of grace—beyond the grace that led God to spare Noah and his family. In spite of human sin (which deserves death), God will not bring humans to an end.

God then proclaims a "sign," which will remind God of his commitment:

And God said, "This is the sign of the covenant I am making between me and you and every living creature with you, a covenant for all generations to come: I have set my rainbow in the clouds, and it will be the sign of the covenant between me and the earth. Whenever I bring clouds over the earth and the rainbow appears in the clouds, I will remember my covenant between me and you and all living creatures of every kind. Never again will the waters become a flood to destroy all life. Whenever the rainbow appears in the clouds, I will see it and remember the everlasting covenant between God and all living creatures of every kind on earth." So God said to Noah, "This is the sign of the covenant I have established between me and all life on the earth." (Gen 9:12-17)

Because this covenant is the first one explicitly mentioned in Scripture, the rainbow is the first sign of a covenant. Later we will see that circumcision is the sign of the Abrahamic covenant (Gen 17:9-14), the sabbath is the sign of the Mosaic covenant (Ex 31:12-18), and the

Lord's Supper is the sign of the new covenant (Lk 22:20).[4] These signs
are like brands. They serve as a reminder to the covenant partners of
the relationship established between them. In the case of the rainbow,
God says the sign will especially remind God of his commitment to
his creatures, human and all other living creatures, to allow for continuity of creation by not bringing a flood again.

Signs are, not surprisingly, integrally related to the specific character of the covenant they are attached to. In the case of the sign of the
Noahic covenant, the rainbow comes out after the storm, thus sig-
naling the cessation of the flood.[5]

Returning to the theme of this proposition, the covenant is a
product of God's grace. Humanity well deserves to suffer extinction
after its repeated and deep rebellion against the one who created it. Yet
God determines not to bring his creation and its creatures to an end
but to begin anew. The covenant sets the context for the entire flood
narrative. The flood narrative finds its main focus in the covenant
since the latter draws a conclusion to the narrative.

The observed intertextual echoes do come with a dark twist since
humans live in the shadow of the fall. Noah and his sons are not
morally innocent as were humans when first created. Thus, we learn
there is disharmony in creation, between humans and the four classes
of created beings.

> The fear and dread of you will fall on all the beasts of the earth,
> and on all the birds of the sky, on every creature that moves
> along the ground, and on all the fish in the sea; they are given
> into your hands. Everything that lives and moves about will be

---

[4]Interestingly, and for reasons that we do not understand, the Davidic covenant (2 Samuel 7)
does not have a sign connected to it.

[5]In contrast, when rainbows are attested in celestial divination texts, they are malefic signs
in five out of eight occurrences. W. Horowitz, "All About Rainbows," in *Laws of Heaven—
Laws of Nature: Legal Interpretations of Cosmic Phenomena in the Ancient World*, ed.
K. Schmid and C. Uehlinger, OBO 276 (Göttingen: Vandenhoeck and Ruprecht, 2016),
40-51.

food for you. Just as I gave you the green plants, I now give you everything. (Gen 9:2-3)

This dark twist also surrounds the language of the image of God, a rare topic in the Old Testament, but one that connects Genesis 1 and 9. In the latter, however, reference to the image is connected to the topic of murder, when God tells Noah and his sons:

Whoever sheds human blood,
> by humans shall their blood be shed;
for in the image of God
> has God made mankind. (Gen 9:6)

Theologians have heard these intertextual echoes and have noted the nature of the relationship between God and the first humans in Genesis 2—where there is a command not to eat of the fruit of the tree of the knowledge of good and evil, with the threat of punishment—and have suggested, though the term is not used, that it is appropriate to refer to the relationship between Adam and God as a covenant of creation. This would receive more support for those who consider Adam and Eve selected to serve a specific role in the garden. If so, then we should refer to the Noahic covenant as a covenant of re-creation. Again, God in his grace gives humanity a new start in the aftermath of the flood. And he commits himself to maintaining humanity and the rest of creation regardless.

Excursus: Genealogies

The stories in Genesis 1–11 are connected by various genealogies (for instance, Gen 4:17–5:32; 10; 11:10-26; there are also genealogies elsewhere in Genesis [36:9-30]). The genealogies therefore contribute to the rhetorical strategy and warrant brief comment. We propose that they imply historical interests but cannot be used to determine chronology. Ancient Near Eastern genealogies aren't constructed for purely

genetic-historical purposes. Remember we need to read these genealogies in their cognitive environment, and not with modern expecta-
tions. That said, while we may not be able to read them as we read
modern genealogies, evidence from the ANE suggests that the names
in genealogies are generally considered real people in a real past.

Analysis of genealogies from the ancient world suggests they are
fluid; that is, they can change in order to reflect contemporary social
realities and perspectives. In the first place, ancient genealogies do not
intend to be exhaustive, so we cannot just "do the math" to get back
from Abram to Noah to Adam. Well over a hundred years ago the
Princeton Old Testament scholar W. H. Green showed that genealogies skip generations by comparing genealogies that cover the same
period of time (1 Chron 6:3-14 and Ezra 7:1-5, for instance).[6] We can
also see the skipping of generations in the genealogy of Jesus in
Matthew 1 when we compare it with the history of the monarchy in
the book of Kings (the former skips Ahaziah [2 Kings 8:25], Joash
[2 Kings 12:1], and Amaziah [2 Kings 14:1]). Green's argument convinced his colleague in theology, B. B. Warfield, the architect of the
modern doctrine of inerrancy, who thus was quite comfortable with
the old age of the earth science pointed to.[7]

In perhaps the most important study of Old Testament genealogies
in the light of ANE analogues, Robert R. Wilson concluded that

> genealogies are not normally created for historical purposes.
> They are not intended to be strictly historical records. Rather
> in the Bible, as well as in the ancient Near Eastern literature
> and in the anthropological material, genealogies seem to have

---

[6]William Henry Green, "Primeval Chronology," *BSac* 47 (1890): 285-303. For a modern assessment, see Ronald L. Numbers, "The Most Important Biblical Discovery of Our Time:
William Henry Green and the Demise of Ussher's Chronology," *Church History* 69 (2000):
257-76.
[7]B. B. Warfield, "On the Antiquity and Unity of the Human Race," *Princeton Theological
Review* 9 (1911): 1-16.

been created for domestic, political-jural, and religious purposes, and historical information is preserved in the genealogies
only incidentally.[8]

They are designed to give people an understanding of their identity.

That genealogies, while including lists of real people in a real past,
are first and foremost making theological statements can be seen by
comparing the genealogies of Jesus in Luke and Matthew, which are
quite different. In addition, the theological interest of Luke's genealogy
is seen when it concludes that Jesus is "the son of Adam, the son of
God" (Lk 3:23-38). As John Nolland puts it, Luke concludes his genealogy of Jesus not with Adam but with God for theological and not
historical reasons:

> Luke would have us see that Jesus takes his place in the human
> family and thus in its (since Adam's disobedience) flawed
> sonship; however, in his own person, in virtue of his unique
> origin (Luke 1:35) but also as worked out in his active obedience
> (4:1-13), he marks a new beginning to sonship and sets it on an
> entirely new footing. In this human situation Jesus is the one
> who is really the Son of God.[9]

Moving Toward the Patriarchal Narratives
(Genesis 11:27–37:2)

God's commitment to the preservation and maintenance of creation
order faces an immediate threat in the aftermath of the covenant he
makes with Noah on behalf of the creation. After the flood, humans
continue to sin (Gen 11:1-9). People unite to build a city and a tower

---

[8]Robert R. Wilson, *Genealogy and History in the Biblical World* (New Haven, CT: Yale University Press, 1977), 199. Also see Marshall D. Johnson, *The Purpose of Biblical Genealogies*,
2nd ed. (Eugene, OR: Wipf & Stock, 2002). For a summary of the state of the discussion,
see John Walton, "Genealogies," in *Dictionary of the Old Testament: Historical Books*, ed. B.
Arnold and H. G. M. Williamson (Downers Grove, IL: InterVarsity Press, 2005), 309-16.
[9]John Nolland, *Luke 1–9:20*, WBC (Nashville: Thomas Nelson, 1989), 173.

that offends God (see proposition thirteen). With this final story, we
have a departure from our pattern, however, since there is no obvious
token of grace in the story itself. The departure from the pattern found
in the stories of Genesis 4–11 prepares us for the next major section of
Genesis, the patriarchal narratives (11:27–37:2), which begins with the
call of Abram (soon Abraham):

> Go from your country, your people and your father's
> household to the land I will show you.
>
> I will make you into a great nation,
>   and I will bless you;
> I will make your name great,
>   and you will be a blessing.
> I will bless those who bless you,
>   and whoever curses you I will curse;
> and all peoples on earth
>   will be blessed through you. (Gen 12:1-3)

God thus initiates a new strategy of carrying out his plans and purposes beginning with this one man and his wife, Sarah; through their
descendants he will reach the world in order to restore blessing on his
human creatures.

Notice the dramatic change in the narrative at this point. Whereas
the primeval narrative covers the whole world over what must be an
incredibly long period of time, now the focus in the second part, the
patriarchal narratives, focuses on one individual—Abraham, then
Jacob, then Joseph—and devotes considerable narrative space to a
relatively short period of time. We observe that such a shift signals a
more intense interest in the details of the events associated with the
patriarchs as founding figures of the people of God.

For our purposes, this understanding of the structure and contents
of the book of Genesis informs us of the importance of interpreting

the flood story in the context of the book of Genesis as a whole, and most especially in the immediate context of Genesis 1–11. So, as we read Genesis 1–11, including the flood story, we believe the genre signals are telling us that these past events (creation, fall, flood, Tower of Babel) actually happened.

In summary, the book of Genesis as a whole shows an interest in the past, but as is often true concerning narratives about the past, its interest is more in the narrator's present. That is why we have adopted the genre label "theological history" to describe the genre of the book of Genesis as a whole, since it is interested in talking about God as he interacts with his people in space and time.[10] What can be learned about the past is of great significance for the literature's present. The most important continuity and unity that characterize Genesis is not one of genre or even of a focus on history but the common theme that unites the book. Having developed the theological pattern that structures the narratives of Genesis 1–11, we now turn our attention to another related pattern developed by the narrator in Genesis 1–11.

---

[10]Tremper Longman III, *Genesis*, SGBC (Grand Rapids: Zondervan, 2016).

The Theological History Is Focused on the Issue of Divine Presence, the Establishment of Order, and How Order Is Undermined

Genesis 1–11 can also be understood as framed by the concepts of divine presence and the order that it brings. Genesis 1–2 describes the identity of the cosmos in terms of being ordered as a place for divine presence followed by the establishment of his presence in Eden. Once people lose access to God's presence, they desire to regain it, as evidenced in Genesis 4:26, where calling on the name of the Lord is invoking divine presence; Genesis 6:1-4, where divine presence is represented in the sons of God (proposition twelve); and Genesis 11:1-9, where the tower is built to facilitate divine presence (proposition thirteen).

Divine presence in the ancient world has significance not just in regard to enabling relationship of some sort between humans and deity but as that which brings and maintains order in the world and in the cosmos. God is the center and source of order; in and through his presence the whole cosmos coheres.[1] Though Genesis 1–11 is

---

[1] Importantly, said also of Jesus in Colossians 1.

framed by the element of divine presence, the driving theme through this section is order, which derives from the divine presence.

In the beginning there was nonorder (Heb. *tohu wabohu* [Gen 1:2]). This condition is not evil or flawed; it is just a work in process. Order in the ancient world defined existence and is characterized by having a purpose (whether in human terms or in the larger sphere of God's plans as much as they could be perceived). Material objects (such as the sea or the desert) in the ancient world could be considered nonexistent if their role and purpose could not be identified by people or if they had no function in human experience.

In the ancient cultural river, the primary act of creation was ordering the cosmos as well as human society.[2] This included activities like naming and separating, and Israelites would have shared this perspective. In God's creative acts, he brought order into the midst of nonorder, but in that process he did not totally dispel nonorder. His plan was that people in his image would work alongside him to continue the order-bringing process (reflected, for example, in "subdue and rule"). Nevertheless, it was all very good—understanding that the point is not that all was perfection but all was able to function the way that God intended at this stage in this ordered system. Consequently, the cosmos at the end of the seven-day account retains some of the nonorder but is characterized by an optimal order that will be maintained and sustained by the presence of God. When he rests, he not only completes this initial phase of ordering (Heb. *shabbat* in Gen 2:1-3) but also takes up his residence in the cosmos he will rule from (Eden in Gen 2; Heb. *nwh* in Ex 20:8-11 and Ps 132:14).[3]

In Genesis 3, this optimally ordered cosmos is disrupted by a third element: disorder, an inherently evil element in that it stands in

---

[2]This follows logically: if order defines existence, and creating something means bringing it into existence, then creation entails ordering.

[3]All of this is worked out in detail in John Walton, *The Lost World of Genesis One* (Downers Grove, IL: InterVarsity Press, 2009).

opposition to the order and presence of God. Disorder results when people decide they want to be like God (attempted by taking from the tree of the knowledge of good and evil). In this they desire to make themselves the center and source of order rather than partnering with God in his order-bringing work. By in effect saying, "I want to do it myself," they set themselves up as an alternate center of order. When they do so, they are cast from God's presence and sent out into the less-ordered world where they will try to proceed on their own. Understandably, success is difficult to achieve and consequently all creation groans in its state of being between order and nonorder as well as subject to the effects of human disorder. It is common for people to think that we live in a world of dichotomy between good and evil. The previous interpretation suggests a further nuance: that we live in a trichotomous world: nonorder (still to be resolved), order, and disorder (evil, the results of sin).

These concepts frame our understanding of the coherence of Genesis 1–11. When we try to understand the coherence of a biblical book (or section of it), we do so by trying to identify the rhetorical strategy that drives the compilation. Episodes were carefully chosen from among many possibilities. The narration of those episodes was presented with purposes in mind. The most acceptable interpretation of that rhetorical strategy is determined by how well it accounts for all of the pieces (both included and omitted) and for the way each episode is presented.

We are now obligated to demonstrate how that explains the choices and shape of the text before us. This is particularly important for this volume since the flood is in the center of Genesis 1–11 and can be understood in the context of the trichotomy we have proposed. What follows is an overview of how Genesis 1–11 traces the trichotomy. Particular pieces of this outline will be picked up in later propositions and dealt with in more detail (specifically, the sons of God episode [proposition twelve] and the Tower of Babel episode [proposition thirteen]).

After ordering the cosmos to be sacred space (Gen 1; "sacred space" is the result of God's presence) and then setting up Eden as the place of his residence (and therefore as sacred space), access to that sacred space is lost when Adam and Eve decide they want to be the center of order. From this point on, people consistently follow their inclinations toward making themselves the center of order, which instead leads to increasing disorder. God responds with correctives that are order bringing. Though sin and its resultant disorder have been introduced, that negative impact is overshadowed by the larger reality that people have lost access to God's presence.

In Genesis 4 it is evident that Cain and Abel are seeking to remain in contact with God as they offer their sacrificial gifts (by the label given to their gifts, *minhah* [offering], they are clearly not thinking of dealing with sin but of retaining God's favor). Sacrifice here is a relationship-building activity but a poor substitute for divine presence. It becomes evident, however, that Cain does not have God's order in mind when he rejects God's offer of a way to gain favor and chooses instead to seek order for himself by killing his brother. Thus he pursues disorder as he seeks his own benefit.

The result is that God banishes him (the thrust of the Hebrew word *'arur*, translated "under a curse" in Gen 4:11). Being driven away from society and the provision of the ground places him in further non-order. Cain notes this by the three things he has lost: provision of the land, access to the presence of God (further reduced), and protection of society (Gen 4:14). Nevertheless, he retains the order that was established in the blessing of Genesis 1:28—he is able to be fruitful and multiply (Gen 4:17).

The genealogical tracing of his line focuses on how human order was established by his descendants. It includes city building (Gen 4:17, a human center of order), animal domestication, musical instruments, and metalworking. In other ancient societies these would have been seen as the developments of the gods or the gifts of the gods. Here they

are represented as human achievements by the line that came from
Cain. In contrast to these accomplishments in human ordering, we
also receive a glimpse of the persistent disorder personified in the
boast of Lamech (Gen 4:23-24). Here we find a warped perspective on
the vengeance God offered in protection of Cain. With Lamech it is
reflected as a right to his own vengeance as he builds order around
himself. So even as order progresses, disorder also becomes en-
trenched and is rationalized with self-justification.

When Genesis 4:25-26 returns to Seth's line, we find that from the
start those who had lost access to the presence of God in the garden
seek its restoration. The phrase "At that time people began to call on
the name of the LORD" is more than just a reference to prayer. It is
typically used of those who are invoking God's presence.[4] Seth's genealogy in Genesis 5 contrasts to Cain's in that it draws attention to
positive examples related to God's presence and order. This explains
the beginning reference to the blessing of God and the image of God
(Gen 5:1-3); attention given to Enoch, who enjoyed the presence of
God in an extraordinary way (Gen 5:22-24); and the naming of
Noah (Gen 5:28-29). Every time Genesis 4–5 steps out of the formula
of the genealogies, it is to make a comment related to order or
presence. The genealogies provide the framework for those narrative asides, even as they document the continuing blessing of God
(being fruitful and multiplying) and the results of sin ("and then he
died"), the ultimate contrast between the results of order and of
nonorder/disorder.

The naming of Noah (Gen 5:29) is of particular importance with
regard to this theme and fairly bristles with intertextuality. The text
indicates that Lamech named his son *noah* (from *nwh*, the Hebrew
word for rest) as an expression of the hope that he would *comfort* us
(Heb. root *nhm* in Piel stem) from our work and from the toil

---

[4]Gen 12:8; 13:4; 21:33; 26:25; 1 Kings 18:24; Ps 116:4.

(Heb. *'itsebon*, used elsewhere only in Gen 3:16, 17) of our hands from the ground (the addition of hands and ground indicates that it is referring to 3:17), which Yahweh "cursed" (Heb. root *'rr*, used in Gen 3:14, 17; 4:11). The root *'rr* refers to a disenfranchising rather than to placing a hex on something; disenfranchisement is inherently order disrupting. In Genesis 3:17 when God does this to the ground, it indicates that people are going to find the ground less usable for growing food. This is a description of the idea that people have now been relegated to a less-ordered realm.[5]

The root *nhm* in the Piel stem is almost always used in cases of mourning when people have reason to be sad but someone comes to console them or offer sympathy. It is an action that seeks to restore some order or stability in a context where nonorder (such as death or destruction) has brought disruption (note Ps 23:4, "your rod and your staff, they *comfort* me"). It is accomplished when honor is restored (Ps 71:21) and by God's love (*hesed*, Ps 119:76). The oppressed are lacking it (Eccles 4:1). Importantly, when God's anger turns away, the result is this comfort (Is 12:1), found in restoration (Is 40:1). All of this relates to Noah in significant ways. Someone who brings comfort (*nhm*) restores order (*nwh*, the root of Noah's name). Significantly, in Akkadian, the cognate root to Hebrew *nwh* is *nahu*, which refers not only to rest but also to relenting.[6] The fact that an Akkadian word pulls together the two different Hebrew verbs associated with Noah's name suggests the account is rooted in Akkadian. This is not the same as saying that the biblical author borrowed from a Mesopotamian account, but that aspects of the account took shape in an Akkadian-language context.

---

[5]In like manner the serpent is banished from its natural group ("from the beasts of the field") in the same way that Cain is banished from his social context, from the production of the ground, and from God's presence—all of the elements that brought order.

[6]*CAD* N 143; noted also by Lloyd R. Bailey, *Noah: The Person and the Story in History and Tradition* (Columbia: University of South Carolina Press, 1989), 168. The word occurs in the Gilgamesh Epic 11.131 to describe the sea relenting, calming down.

With this understanding of the vocabulary used and the information about the other passages in the near context where the same vocabulary is used, we are in a position to get a sense of the meaning of this verse. The naming of Noah could indicate that he will be the one through whom order is preserved and restored in the aftermath of the insurgence of nonorder represented in the flood. Be that as it may, however, the text indicates that Noah would comfort us (presumably humankind) "*from* our labor and *from* the toil of our hands *from* the ground" (authors' translation). The combination of the verb *nhm* with the preposition *min* (from) occurs three times in this verse and nowhere else in the Hebrew Bible. The combination does not suggest consolation or comfort *concerning* those things—that uses a different preposition. It can mean only that nonorder related to the labor, toil, and ground are going to be resolved and a greater semblance of order would be restored. It is difficult to deduce *how* that is taking place; what is important is that *it is* taking place. The vocabulary shows us how the flood is being interpreted—it is an order-bringing event.[7] The connection of Noah's name to the flood suggests that besides being presented as an act of judgment, grace, and deliverance, the narrator is recounting this event as a sort of order "reset button." God uses nonorder (the waters) to eliminate disorder (pervasive violence) and then to reestablish optimal order (even as he recognizes that disorder remains [Gen 8:21]).[8]

---

[7]It is of interest that the names of the flood heroes in the ANE flood stories (Ziusudra/Utanapishti = "He found life"; Atrahasis [more a title than a name] = "exceedingly wise," actually used in the Gilgamesh Epic 11.197) also make reference to the hero's significance in light of the flood. For analysis of the former, see Andrew George, *The Babylonian Gilgamesh Epic* (Oxford: Oxford University Press, 2003), 1:152-53; for the latter, see Jeffrey H. Tigay, *Evolution of the Gilgamesh Epic* (Philadelphia: University of Pennsylvania Press, 1982), 229.

[8]Note Anne Draffkorn Kilmer, "Of Babies, Boats, and Arks," in *Studies Presented to Robert Biggs*, ed. M. Roth et al. (Chicago: Oriental Institute, 2007), 159-65, who collects the information demonstrating that a boat is used repeatedly as a uterine symbol, thus recognizing the ark in Genesis as a vessel that contained the seed of all life being prepared for rebirth.

Making connections such as these not only serves to draw out the internal coherence of Genesis 1–11 (literarily and theologically) but also must lead to an understanding of how Genesis 1–11 functions in the larger book. We agree with the idea that has been articulated in many ways throughout the history of interpretation that Genesis 1–11 serves as an essential introduction to the covenant. It explains the need for a covenant and helps put it in perspective to establish what the covenant is all about.

Such a role has some similarity to a literary phenomenon observable repeatedly in ANE literature, where it is common for narratives about primeval time to set the stage for a narrated history.[9] If Genesis 12–50 stands as the primary narrated history, which we believe it does, Genesis 1–11 serves the purpose of providing a prologue using illustrations from primeval history. Furthermore, the flood account in the ANE literature is used not only as part of these primeval prologues but also in destruction-restoration contexts that are leading to a new order. In Genesis the new order is represented first of all in the re-creation following the flood, but more importantly in the covenant story that frames the ancestor narratives. We will discuss this relationship further in proposition twelve.

We have noted in the chapters that precede the flood narrative the disintegration of order is documented. This stands in contrast to what we observe in the narratives that precede the flood in the Atrahasis Epic. There, order disintegration is not manifested in human behavior; instead, the gods are engaged in repeated attempts to reduce the population because of their discontent with humans. This, along with other comparisons to the ANE accounts, was discussed in proposition eight.

We have suggested that the purpose of Genesis 1–11 is to trace the establishment of order, dissolution of order, and reconstitution of order, related to the presence of God, as an introduction to the covenant. As

---

[9]For example, see Yi Samuel Chen, *The Primeval Flood Catastrophe* (Oxford: Oxford University Press, 2013), 68-69.

delineated section by section, the elements of order and presence can be seen as the editor of Genesis 1–11 selects and presents his material. This interpretation is demonstrated by the intertextual connections between Genesis 1–3 and Genesis 6–9 (see proposition ten). Here we develop the literary-theological pattern that unfolds when the creation/re-creation idea is seen in light of the nonorder-order-disorder paradigm.

Genesis 1 began with nonorder consisting of water and darkness. God's creative work brought order by establishing roles and functions in accordance with his purpose. In Genesis 6–8 there is a recurrence of the nonordered condition by means of the floodwaters, and a re-establishment of order. Furthermore, an indication is given that there was a greater permanence to the cosmos's order (Gen 8:21-22). The covenant in Genesis 9:8-17 reiterates the blessing in similar terms to how order had been restored to the cosmos in Genesis 8. Just as Genesis 8:21-22 indicated God would not interfere with the ordered cosmos in such a way again, so Genesis 9:15 indicates that neither would he interfere with the blessing in such a way. Table 1 summarizes the intertextual connections.

Table 1. Intertextual connections between Genesis 1–3 and Genesis 6–9

ITEMS	GENESIS 1–3	GENESIS 6–9
Nonordered cosmos	1:2	7:17-24
Order established in the cosmos	1:3–2:4	8:1-22 (without further interference)
Blessing given	1:26-30	9:1-8
Blessing nonfunctional	2:5-6	7:17-24
Blessing renewed	2:7-24	9:9-17 (without further interference)
Plant connected with fall	2:9	9:20
Naked and unaware	2:25	9:21
Offense related to blessing boundaries	3:1-6	9:22-23
Eyes were opened and knew	3:7	9:24
Pronouncement	3:14-19	9:25-27

The flood account specifically has the role of showing how God reestablished order after bringing the waters of the nonordered cosmos to wipe out the disorder that had come to dominate the antediluvian world. In this way the flood account recapitulates creation. That is why the narrator includes the story. He is showing how God had worked to bring about order in the past (creation and flood). This serves as an introduction to Yahweh's strategy to advance order yet again through the covenant. The covenant is an order-bringing strategy using the mechanisms of election, relationship, and revelation as the foundation for reestablishing his presence on earth (initially through the tabernacle).

As noted in proposition nine, if we wish to get to the core of the authority of the author, we have to focus on what the author (who has been vested with God's authority) is doing with the event. We now have that purpose before us, and we can understand the authoritative message of the text without having to know how to reconstruct the event itself. Before we proceed to modern conversations about the flood (e.g., geology and flood traditions around the world), we need to discuss two more narratives from Genesis 1–11 in order to understand their role in the rhetorical strategy.

The "Sons of God" Episode Is Not Only a Prelude to the Flood; It Is the Narrative Sequel to Cain and Abel

Both of us have written commentaries on Genesis and have outlined the various perspectives on the "sons of God" episode promoted throughout the history of interpretation.[1] Theological interpretation among Christian writers from the second century onward generally adopted a view that the sons of God were those from the line of Seth indiscriminately marrying those from the ungodly line of Cain. Rabbinic interpreters were more inclined to see the offending party as kings engaged in polygamy. Both of these have been demonstrated to be unlikely when subjected to scrutiny.[2] Attention to the ancient Near East has resulted in the idea that kings in the ancient world styled themselves as divinely conceived (thus sons of God) and were known to practice the "right of the first night" (as in the Gilgamesh Epic),

---

[1]Tremper Longman III, *Genesis*, SGBC (Grand Rapids: Zondervan, 2016); John H. Walton, *Genesis*, NIVAC (Grand Rapids: Zondervan, 2001); and John H. Walton, "Genesis," in *Zondervan Illustrated Bible Backgrounds Commentary*, ed. John H. Walton (Grand Rapids: Zondervan, 2009). See also John H. Walton, "Sons of God, Daughters of Man," in *Dictionary of the Old Testament: Pentateuch*, ed. T. D. Alexander and D. W. Baker (Downers Grove, IL: InterVarsity Press, 2003), 793-98.
[2]Walton, *Genesis*, 291-95.

taking as wives whomever they chose. In contrast, focus on the use of terminology in the Bible suggests that "sons of God" (as rare as it is) refers consistently to the members of the divine council (e.g., Job 1-2), and this is the interpretation adopted in the earliest sources (Second Temple period works like the Book of Enoch) as well as reflected in the New Testament (2 Peter and Jude).[3] As commentators, we each have our views, but both of us acknowledge a lot of uncertainties in the identification of the parties. For this book, however, the identification of the parties, and even the interpretation of the offense, is less important than the use the narrator is making of the story.

To understand the role the account has in the rhetorical strategy of Genesis 1-11, it is important to recognize a pattern used by the compiler of Genesis. The pattern is reflected in the technique of recursion, which is best understood by citing a couple of examples. In Genesis 25, after recounting the death of Abraham, the narrator is ready to move on to the next stage in the story. Before doing so, he provides the genealogy of Ishmael (Gen 25:12-18). This genealogy pushes forward in time well beyond the period of the ancestors, but then the narrator steps back to the story of Isaac represented in Jacob and Esau. This is narrative recursion—moving forward through time to tie up a loose end, then coming back to the main account. It happens again when the genealogies of Esau are followed (Gen 36) before the narrator returns to the story of Jacob's sons. The technique of recursion is also evident in Genesis 1-11. Most notably, after the story of the flood, Noah's sons are tracked through their respective lines in which the languages of the world develop, and then the narrator turns back in time to when the world still had one language—the account of the Tower of Babel, which we therefore deduce took place soon after the flood. After the Tower of Babel story, the narrator then uses the genealogy of Shem to bridge to the next narrative, the covenant story of Abram.

---

[3]At the same time it must be recognized that the New Testament follows the lead of the Second Temple literature.

We note in each of these the narrative recursion follows a genealogical record that reaches further ahead in time. Based on the observation of how recursion is used routinely in Genesis, we should be willing to apply it yet again to the account of the sons of God in Genesis 6:1-4. As in the other cases, we have a narrative following a genealogy. The genealogy of Cain in Genesis 4:17-24 had been followed by a recursion that returned to Adam and Eve and their new son Seth (Gen 4:25-26). Genesis 5 then contains the Seth genealogy, which leads to Noah. If we follow the pattern of recursion, the narrative of Genesis 6:1-4 then returns to the time after Adam and Seth.[4]

Evidences that it should be read this way are found in the language of the short pericope:

- The account takes place when *ha'adam* ("humanity" with definite article, just as in Gen 5:2) *begins* multiplying.
- The sons of God "saw that the daughters of man were good"[5]—using the same language from Genesis 1 and 3 (God saw that x was good; the woman saw that the fruit was good).

One possible problem with this interpretation is that as a result, the restriction of 120 years, often interpreted as limiting human lifespans, appears to take place *before* the list of long-lived members of the line of Seth. It must be recognized, however, that a similar problem exists if we place the pericope just before the flood, because not only Noah and those in Shem's genealogy but also Abraham, Isaac, and Jacob all continue to live longer lives. At the same time, interpreting the 120 years as a reference to human lifespan is not the only option.

An alternative interpretation developed through a reconsideration of the biblical text as well as information from ANE usage considers the 120 years to be a period of time for humanity's survival until the

---

[4]This interpretation is the result of questions raised by John's student Scott Cunningham in a Genesis class and the subsequent brainstorming discussion by the class.
[5]This is not the normal Hebrew word for beautiful.

flood. First, with regard to the text, Genesis 6:3 indicates that God's spirit (*ruah*) is in some way going to be removed prior to the 120 years.[6] It is stated in the verse that the spirit is going to be removed from humanity (*ha'adam*), and in Zechariah 12:1 we discover that Yahweh forms the spirit of (corporate) humanity. When God's spirit is removed, the result is death. Consequently, the verse can be understood to refer to a span of 120 years before (corporate) humanity will lose God's spirit and die.

Such a reference to time spans also occurs preceding the flood in the Atrahasis Epic. There, after the creation of humanity (corporate), "1,200 years had not yet passed, when the land extended and the peoples multiplied"; already problems developed between humanity and the gods (see proposition 8—here its description does not matter). The gods send disease to reduce the population, but humans are coached to respond by withholding food from the gods in general while giving gifts to the god of disease, who then relents. Again, 1,200 years had not yet passed, the problem continues, and the gods send drought and its resulting famine. Again, humans respond by building a temple to the storm god and bringing him gifts, and the god relents.

The similarity that is important at this point is that the gods undertake strategies to address the human disorder that are separated by a set, formulaic period of time and eventuate in a flood. The flood is not only judgment on humans but a strategy designed to bring order to the cosmos (which in Mesopotamia means order for the gods). The 120 years of the biblical narrative also then could be considered to represent a set period of time before the remedy of the flood is sent to restore cosmic order.[7]

---

[6]The verb that expresses what God's spirit is not going to do (*yadon*) remains resistant to analysis.

[7]This 120 is a decimal representation that perhaps could be compared to the 1,200, which is in the sexagesimal notation used in Mesopotamia. Twelve hundred is represented in the Akkadian text of Atrahasis as 600.600.

We still have the problem, however, that if the narrative is placed in the time period of Seth, 120 years can hardly be considered the time that will elapse until the flood, given all the long lives in Seth's line. We would propose, then, that the description of what is going on between the sons of God and daughters of men (whoever they are) extends throughout the period of Seth's genealogy. In other words, this is the way the biblical text characterizes the entire ante-diluvian period,[8] and at some point toward the end of that period, the 120-year ultimatum is given. The "sons of God" era begins at the time of Seth, continues through the antediluvian period when the Nephilim and great heroes dominated (whoever they are and whatever their biological relationship to the sons of God), and draws to a conclusion at the time of Noah, with the assessment of the entire period being given in Yahweh's soliloquy in Genesis 6:5-8. Noah's story then picks up with the *toledot* introduction in Genesis 6:9.

In this view, the sons of God marrying the daughters of men (inter-mixing what ought not to be mixed) is not identified as the cause of the flood. It is simply part of the antediluvian landscape (a primordial era), along with the Nephilim and heroes of old, that contributes to the escalation of violence and corruption in that world (evidenced, for example, by Lamech in Gen 4:23-24). The flood is not framed in Genesis as judgment on the sons of God; it is reestablishing order from the disorder that has been escalating. Without the life-giving spirit of God (which sustains life), humanity dies as the flood wipes them from the face of the earth to start anew.

Further interesting connections for understanding this passage and the era it characterizes are suggested when we compare elements from the ANE literature and the Second Temple period literature about the antediluvian period. In Mesopotamian lore there are individuals in

---

[8]This is similar to what we find in the book of Judges, where the entire Judges period is characterized by "In those days Israel had no king; everyone did as they saw fit."

the antediluvian period called the *apkallu*.[9] These are generally considered semidivine creatures who are the great sages most well-known for bringing the arts of civilization to humanity from the gods. In this latter role they correspond to those in Cain's genealogy. The most famous of the *apkallu* is Adapa, who offended the gods and, as a result, was denied immortality. Adapa is identified as a "son of [the god] Ea."[10] Though the *apkallu* are never corporately referred to as "sons of God," in the book of Enoch (second century BC) the "Watchers" are the sons of God, parents of the Nephilim, and the ones who brought the arts of civilization to humanity. The book of Enoch therefore has the Watchers in the same role as both the Mesopotamian *apkallu* and the sons of God in Genesis 6.[11] Psalm 82 may add one more piece to this puzzle. There God addresses the "great assembly" (the divine council who are elsewhere the "sons of God") and reprimands them for their failure to maintain justice. In verse 6 these "gods" are referred to as "sons of the Most High," who will nevertheless die as mortals (bringing to mind Gen 6:3). This could feasibly be understood as related to the primordial, antediluvian era introduced in Genesis 6:1-4.

The four-way connection between Genesis 6, Psalm 82, the Mesopotamian *apkallu*, and the Enochian Watchers, tenuous as it may be, invites an interpreter to use these diverse sources together as mutually informing. Such an interpretation would co-identify the sons of God, *apkallu*, and Watchers as the same group. This group intermarries with human women (true of all three groups)[12] and, though intended to

---

[9]Anne Draffkorn Kilmer, "The Mesopotamian Counterparts of the Biblical Nephilim," in *Perspectives on Language and Text*, ed. Edgar W. Conrad and Edward G. Newing (Winona Lake, IN: Eisenbrauns, 1987), 39-44.

[10]It is also of interest that Adapa is often identified by scholars as either Utuabzu or Enmeduranki, the seventh among the *apkallu*, who "ascended to heaven" (compared perhaps to Enoch). See A. Annus, "On the Origin of Watchers: A Comparative Study of the Antediluvian Wisdom in Mesopotamian and Jewish Traditions," *Journal for the Study of the Pseudepigrapha* 19 (2010): 280.

[11]Ibid., 277-320.

[12]Postflood *ummianu* are two-thirds *apkallu*, indicating that the latter mated with human women; see ibid., 282.

extend order, instead initiates an era of corruption and injustice perpetrated by them and their offspring. The *apkallu* can be seen as connected to the gods because they are considered those who direct the plans of heaven and earth—a divine task. They are therefore agents of order whose influence eventually brought disorder. Lamech (in Cain's genealogy) would be one of their number.

In conclusion, this episode can now be seen in light of the overall rhetorical strategy in Genesis 1–11. It documents a quasi-presence of God represented in the sons of God. But that form of presence is rejected by God—it resulted in further disorder, not order. When we take a careful look at the account of the Tower of Babel (next proposition), we will see that it also involves a failed initiative to restore God's presence. This literary-theological role of the account can be affirmed despite our inability to determine the identity of the main players or the meaning of key words.

Proposition 13

The Tower of Babel (Genesis 11:1-9) Is an Appropriate Conclusion to the Primeval Narrative

It should first be noted that the account of the Tower of Babel has authentic roots in the period that ranges from the end of the fourth millennium through the first quarter of the third millennium BC. In terms of the technologies referred to, burned brick technology was unique to Mesopotamia, where the location in the alluvial plains would have required stones to be imported over great distances and only at great expense. As a more expedient alternative, bitumen mortar was commonly used with kiln-fired brick. This technology is first attested in the late Uruk period and becomes more common in the Jemdat Nasr period, thus dating to the end of the fourth millennium. This technology was used in public buildings and at the beginning of urbanization. Cities of this period comprised public buildings only, primarily the temple complex.

ZIGGURAT TOWER

The tower was a ziggurat—of that there is little doubt.[1] In ANE texts it is common to describe a ziggurat as built "with its head in the heavens." Furthermore, the chronological and geographical context suggests the well-known ziggurats of southern Mesopotamia, where they were the dominant feature of the city. Ziggurat architecture featured a brick structure filled with rubble—that is, unlike a pyramid, there were no interior spaces. These structures were the visible center of the temple complex but served a peripheral function in sacred space, where the true center was the adjoining temple. The ziggurat and the temple served as a cosmic portal, bridging the gap between the realms. The names given to the ziggurats confirmed this ideology. In their cosmic role they provided a convenience for the gods as the tower invited them to descend into the temple to be worshiped. We are reminded of a modern executive elevator. Importantly, and against the history of interpretation, such a structure did not provide a way for humans to ascend, as Genesis 11:5 itself attests, but for gods to descend. Ziggurats were part of sacred space and inaccessible to the public. They were not temples per se, because there were no rituals performed there and no image of deity was resident there, but they were considered part of sacred space, and thus their names were prefaced with the same Sumerian designations as the temples. The ziggurat was a stairway *from* heaven.

BIBLICAL TEXT

The most significant interpretational issues are centered on the phrases "make ourselves a name" and "lest we be scattered." We can briefly deal with the latter before giving more attention to the former. It is not difficult to determine that desiring not to scatter was natural.

---

[1] Andrew George, *House Most High: The Temples of Ancient Mesopotamia* (Winona Lake, IN: Eisenbrauns, 1993); Thorkild Jacobsen, "Notes on Ekur," *EI* 21 (1990): 40-47; and Julian Reade and Irving Finkel, "The Ziggurat and Temples of Nimrud," *Iraq* 64 (2002): 135-216.

In Genesis 13 Abram and Lot did not want to separate, but circumstances demanded it. Scattered families bring discontinuity and disrupt relationship and traditions being passed on. The need for scattering was somewhat resolved through urbanization, which city building addressed. The need to scatter due to limited food inhibited order; building a city represented an attempt to bring increased order to their lives.

Consequently, contrary to a strong tradition to identify the offense of the builders as disobedience to the creation mandate ("fill the earth"), we must note that for there to be disobedience, there must be a command. No connection should be drawn to the creation mandate in Genesis 1, because "filling" is accomplished by reproduction, not by geographical dispersion. Furthermore, the so-called creation mandate is not a command but a blessing, and cannot be disobeyed.[2]

Regarding making a name, it is important to recognize it was naturally desirable for people to achieve that objective, and it was not intrinsically prideful. It was accomplished by anything that resulted in one being remembered. It *could* be motivated by pride but was perhaps more importantly associated with the idea that a person might benefit in the afterlife by their name being remembered. While conquests or great building projects could accomplish that end, so could having children.[3] The building project in this passage would certainly qualify to make a name for the builders, but it is more difficult to identify the desire to make a name as an offense to God.

In order to understand the offensive nature of the project, we have to dip into the cognitive environment of the ancient world. We have previously introduced the concept of the Great Symbiosis to describe the system wherein the gods had created humanity to meet their needs,

---

[2]It is true that the verb *fill* is imperative, but *command* is only one possible function of imperative forms. In Genesis 1 we are specifically told that the illocution is a blessing; blessings are not commands.

[3]For affirmation of these ideas see Karen Radner and Eleanor Robson, *Oxford Handbook of Cuneiform Culture* (Oxford: Oxford University Press, 2011), 113-14.

which was the goal of the rituals of the ancient world (proposition eight). In turn, the gods met the needs of humanity (provision and protection). This symbiosis results in codependence and is contrary to the biblical ideal in which Yahweh has no needs. Great Symbiosis thinking, which pervaded the religious systems in the ancient world, was based on mutual needs.

The relationship between the Great Symbiosis and the ziggurat can be recognized through an understanding of the *gigunu*, the shrine at the top of the ziggurat.[4] "It was a rectangular-shaped structure bordered by a reed fence and a stand of [cedar] trees that occupied the top of the ziggurat."[5] The *gigunu* served as the residential quarters for the god when he was not actively involved in temple activities.[6] It is not a place for the image to receive worship or sacrificial rituals. He is "off duty." The inner room in the *gigunu*, called the "room of darkness," is for sleeping. Provisions were also made for food, bathing, or being anointed.

When Great Symbiosis thinking is brought to the context of Genesis 11, we can perceive an important nuance in the builders' desire to make a name for themselves. In the past when this motivation was evaluated, it was often indicated that the builders' offense was in the fact that *they* were trying to make a name for themselves rather than allowing *God* to make a name for them. We propose instead that the contrast is not found in the verbal action (*making* a name rather than *not* making a name) nor in the subject (*them* making a name rather than *God* making a name for them), but in the indirect object (a name for *themselves* rather than for *God*). If sacred space is being constructed (as a ziggurat would suggest), its objective should be making a name for God, not for making a name for themselves. Note, for

---

[4] Thorkild Jacobsen, "The Mesopotamian Temple Plan and the Kititum Temple," *EI* 20 (1989): 78-91; and Jacobsen, "Notes on Ekur," 40-47. In earliest times it was a reed structure erected on an artificial mound (*CAD* G 69).

[5] Jacobsen, "Notes on Ekur," 41.

[6] Similar to a modern-day green room, an offstage accommodation for performers.

example, in Enuma Elish 6.51: "Let us build a sanctuary whose name is famous." Great Symbiosis thinking, however, could easily lead to a motivation focused on their own success and well-being.[7] That is, their motivation for constructing sacred space was to bring benefits to themselves.

The ideal that construction of sacred space ought to make a name for deity is reflected both in the ANE literature, such as in the names of ziggurats or temples,[8] and in the biblical ideology.[9] Such an offense does not represent encroaching on divine boundaries (as has often been suggested as the offense of the builders) as much as diminishing divine attributes. The builders were attempting to establish sacred space, itself a commendable activity, but their motivations were flawed.

At this point it is obvious all the main interpretations of the offense of the tower builders are being called into question: they are not trying to ascend to heaven, they are not ostensibly guilty of pride, and they are not disobeying a command to fill the earth.

The ziggurat was part of a system in which the gods descended to inhabit the image that had been prepared to contain their essence, and through that image the god would be cared for through rituals designed for that purpose. The text does not articulate this system, but it does not need to. The symbol of the ziggurat spoke clearly to Israelites familiar with its function. Jacob's dream in Genesis 28 is further evidence of their understanding.

---

[7]Stimulated by observation by John's student Justin White.

[8]A. George, *House Most High: The Temples of Ancient Mesopotamia* (Winona Lake: Eisenbrauns, 1993), #140: "House of Fame" (*bit dalili*) Nippur; #811: "House of the Exalted Name"; and #812: "House Chosen by Name."

[9]Ps 34:3, exalt (*rum*) the Lord's name, implied from Mal 1:11-12 (if a name can be defiled it can theoretically be made great); building a temple for the "Name of the Lord" (1 Kings 3:2; 5:3-5; 8:16-29).

Comparative Studies: ANE Literature
and the Cognitive Environment

No account found in the literature of the ANE parallels the event portrayed in Genesis 11:1-9, but the pericope is rich in authentic ideas and elements recognizable in the cognitive environment. We will summarize the elements briefly and then discuss what we learn from the comparative exercise.

In ANE literature there is a familiar motif known as the "irreverent king" that typically identifies offense in a particular king whose unsanctioned actions are interpreted as leading to the downfall of a city, dynastic line, or empire. Near the end of what is known as the Ur III dynasty, Amar-Suen (2046–2038 BC), the son of the famous, long-lived Shulgi, was on the throne of Ur and is portrayed as just such an irreverent king.[10] A sequence of events during his reign sounds some familiar themes. Though the political center of the empire was in Ur, the nearby town of Eridu held great religious significance as the center of power for the god Enki. The construction of the temple and ziggurat of Enki at Eridu had been launched by the first king of the dynasty, Ur-Nammu, but he had been unable to complete it.[11] Amar-Suen undertook to complete this project but year after year could not gain the permission of the gods. Usually one of the greatest desires of the gods was to have their temples built, so it was considered a sign of deep consternation for permission not to be granted. Nevertheless, Amar-Suen eventually proceeded (unclear whether he gained permission or not) and, furthermore, explicitly did so "to make his name everlasting."[12]

---

[10]Piotr Michalowski, "Amar-Suena and the Historical Tradition," in *Essays on the Ancient Near East*, ed. M. J. Ellis (Hamden, CT: Archon, 1977), 155-57.

[11]The temple was called the Apsu (é.abzu) and the ziggurat was é.unir (meaning "temple tower"). For more information, see George, *House Most High*, 65, line 30, and p. 154, line 1150.

[12]Peeter Espak, *The God Enki in Sumerian Royal Ideology and Mythology* (Wiesbaden, Germany: Harrassowitz Verlag, 2015), 61. See also the text "Amar-Suena and Enki's Temple" (Amar-Suena A), http://etcsl.orinst.ox.ac.uk/cgi-bin/etcsl.cgi?text=t.2.4.3.1&charenc=j#.

Amar-Suen was succeeded by Shu-Suen and Ibbi-Suen before the dynasty and empire finally fell. The fall of Ur was brought about after decades of disruption attributed to the "Amorites," but the final blow came at the hands of the Elamites. This fall is elegized in two well-known compositions from the ancient world, "Lamentation Over the Destruction of Ur" and "Lamentation Over the Destruction of Sumer and Ur."

The idea that Amar-Suen may have been considered culpable concerning the fall is tenuously drawn from a couple of indicators. In another hymn of Amar-Suen (Hymn B), it indicates that Enki had left his temple in Eridu as a result of problems among the people:

At that time mankind was not [good/put in order?] [. . .]

Far from wisdom, not spe[aking?] intelligent words [. . .]

. . .

Badness was created; to do bad things was good(?)[13]

The sequence of historical events in the last few decades leading up to the fall of the Ur III dynasty is uncertain due to the lack of documents. Some scholars have suggested that Eridu was abandoned as early as the reign of Amar-Suen, or at least that it fell earlier than the city of Ur.[14]

When we tally up the parallels between the situation of Amar-Suen and the Tower of Babel, we find that there is no reason to think they are both referring to the same events or that a particular piece of literature from the ANE ties them together. But the comparison demonstrates that many of the aspects of the Tower of Babel story would have been quite at home in the ancient world context.

---

[13]Espak, *God Enki*, 61.

[14]Dominique Charpin, *Clergé d'Ur au siècle d'Hammurapi* (Paris: Gallimard/NRF, 1986), 294. For discussion, see Espak, *God Enki*, 114. If this is so, it would be intriguing because, though Eridu is generally considered the first city in Mesopotamian traditions, the names Eridu and Babylon are often interchanged in early texts, and in the Eridu Genesis, both refer to the same city. Stephanie Dalley, "Babylon as a Name for Other Cities Including Nineveh," in *Proceedings of the 51st Rencontre Assyriologique Internationale Held at the Oriental Institute of the University of Chicago, July 18-22, 2005*, ed. R. D. Biggs, J. Meyers, and M. T. Roth, RAI 51 (Chicago: University of Chicago, 2008), 25-34, esp. 25-26.

One more intriguing reference from the ancient world is worth mentioning. We have already referred to the *apkallu* in connection to the sons of God in Genesis 6 (proposition twelve). The major *apkallu* tradition is antediluvian, but after the flood there are four *apkallu*, and each one is cited for an offense (angering a particular god with no detail given). The last one, however, is indicted as the one who "brought Ishtar down from heaven into the sanctuary."[15] The idea that the stairways of the ziggurat were meant for the god to come down is evidenced in the Mesopotamian myth "Nergal and Ereshkigal," where the messenger of the gods descends from heaven down to the nether-world by means of a stairway (Akk. *simmiltu*). The connection of this mythical stairway to ziggurats is specified by the name of the ziggurat at Sippar: "Sacred Place of the Pure Stairway to Heaven."[16]

COHERENCE OF GENESIS 1–11

The understanding of the offense as trying to reestablish God's presence with flawed motives leads us to an understanding of the role of the tower-building account in the rhetorical strategy of Genesis 1–11. In Genesis 2 God constructed sacred space in the Garden of Eden. People were placed in sacred space with priestly duties (Gen 2:15). Life and wisdom (represented by the trees) were available in the presence of God. When people, prompted by the serpent, sought to make themselves the center of wisdom and order ("You will be like gods"), they were cast out of the sacred space. In Genesis 4 sacrificial gifts are being brought, and in Genesis 4:26 people began to call on the name of the Lord—but neither of these reestablishes divine presence. Genesis 6:1-4 indicated a lesser substitute for divine presence in the sons of God, whose era stretches from Adam to Noah.

---

[15]A. Annus, "On the Origin of Watchers: A Comparative Study of the Antediluvian Wisdom in Mesopotamian and Jewish Traditions," *Journal for the Study of the Pseudepigrapha* 19 (2010): 297.
[16]George, *House Most High*, 115, #672: é.kun$_4$.an.kù.ga, where Sumerian kun$_4$ = Akkadian *simmiltu*. The Hebrew cognate for *simmiltu*, *sullam*, is the word describing the ladder/ stairway that Jacob sees in his dream, Gen 28:10-12.

Genesis 11:1-9 gives an account of the builders taking initiative to reinitiate sacred space through the abiding presence of God in a temple (associated with the ziggurat), to bring God down and thereby regain a privilege lost at Eden.[17] The theme of Genesis 1–11 is not simply encroachment on divine prerogatives or violation of boundaries between divine and human identities, but the encroachment of disorder on the ordered realm. Adam and Eve brought disorder of sin and death (instigated by a chaos creature, the serpent). We have already traced the development of the theme of order (proposition eleven) and can now add a few more points in the development of that theme across Genesis 1–11:

- Just as creation in Genesis 1 established order, so after the flood, order is reestablished in a recapitulation of creation. Dry land emerged from cosmic waters in Genesis 8 as in Genesis 1. People and animals were brought forth in both, and blessing was given in both. But a key difference is that God has not "rested" in his presence among his people.

- The covenant with Noah after the flood does not repeat "subdue and rule." In Genesis 1 this served as the expression for the human role in extending order. Now, however, extending order based on sacred space and God's presence is no longer possible, but humans are called to maintain social order, which is still a responsibility (e.g., judging capital crimes [Gen 9:6]).

- The Babel project, motivated by the Great Symbiosis, represented disorder in the divine and human interrelationships and resulted in God's interruption of order by the confusion of languages.

- Tower builders conceived of sacred space as focused on themselves (making a name for themselves)—a repetition of the Garden of Eden scenario—thus forming an inclusio to

---

[17]Suggested by John's student Eva Teague.

Genesis 1–11. The motivation of the building project was for order determined by them and built around themselves.

When the theme of order by means of divine presence is recognized in Genesis 1–2, and when the restoration of divine presence is recognized as the motivation of the ziggurat builders, Genesis 1–11 can be seen as a unit with these important bookends serving as a rhetorical inclusio for the record of the primordial period.

Linkage between Genesis 1–11 and Genesis 12–50. The interpretation of Genesis 1–11 we have presented in general, and specifically the interpretation of Genesis 11, not only establishes the thematic, theological continuity across Genesis 1–11 but also provides the basis for the transition from Genesis 1–11 to Genesis 12–50.[18] To see the linkage, we need to examine the conclusion of the Babel narrative, the confusion of tongues and scattering of the people.

In the view of the offense and of the rhetorical strategy of Genesis 1–11 already offered, the confusion of tongues and the resultant scattering can be seen as more than punishment. More precisely, it is a means, not an end in itself. The objective is for the city building to be stopped.[19] God indeed descends (Gen 11:5) as the builders intended, but he is not pleased at their initiative because of the premise it is founded on. They have crossed a threshold (Gen 11:6) by seeking to establish order by means of sacred space and the institution of the Great Symbiosis that sacred space facilitated.

The scattering by means of confusion of tongues sets the stage for the programmatic counterinitiative Yahweh intends. This began in Genesis 10, which describes the rise of the seventy nations; Genesis 11 describes the scattering of the nations. These nations can be recognized as being apportioned to the sons of God in Deuteronomy 32:8.[20] Then

---

[18]Mark A. Awabdy, "Babel, Suspense, and the Introduction to the Terah-Abram Narrative," *JSOT* 35 (2010): 3-29, suggests the idea that Genesis 12 is a response to Genesis 11:1-9.

[19]Stimulated by observation by John's student Ashley Edewaard.

[20]Stimulated by observation by John's student John Raines.

Genesis 12 initiates God's choice of the nation of Israel (again alluded to in Deuteronomy 32:8). Election (covenant) requires diversity (since one is chosen from among many). This then leads us to an examination of the rhetorical relationship of the two major sections of Genesis.

The tower-building account has introduced a second theological problem that needs to be resolved. The first was the sin-disorder problem introduced at the fall, resulting in the loss of access to sacred space. Before those problems can be resolved, it is imperative that God reveals his nature and institutes relationship so sacred space can be reestablished on a proper basis.

In this way the tower-building narrative is followed naturally by God's initiative to reestablish sacred space through his abiding presence. This will happen after he has established a relationship (the covenant) through which he reveals himself (to the ancestors and at Sinai) as a prelude to the construction of sacred space (the tabernacle) on the corrected premise of a ritual system that does not presume a needy deity. He makes a place for his name to be honored. He rejected the builders' flawed strategy and embarks on his own initiative. God's initiative is going to reestablish his presence not on the strength of their unity but in the midst of their diversity; not through the Great Symbiosis characterized by codependence but through the great enterprise of the covenant characterized by the Torah. In this way Genesis 11 offers a bridge to Genesis 12: Genesis 11 is failed human initiative to reestablish God's presence; Genesis 12 is God's initiative that will lead to relationship in his presence and sacred space.[21] This suggests again that Genesis 1–11 serves the function of providing an introduction to the ancestral narratives in Genesis 12–50.

As a last supporting observation, we can compare and contrast Genesis 11 with Jacob's dream in Genesis 28. In Genesis 11 the people

---

[21]Suggested by Eva Teague.

build a ziggurat (stairway) in order to try to bring God down and establish sacred space. In Genesis 28, as part of the process of establishing the covenant, God initiates the coming down (stairway) and the recognition of sacred space (Bethel: this is the house of God!). We see then that Yahweh is moving toward the establishment of his presence (which will be completed when he descends to inhabit the tabernacle) and is now doing so in connection to the covenant. On the basis of all of these literary and theological observations, the covenant can now be recognized as having its focus in the reestablishment of access to God's presence on earth. He will dwell in the midst of his covenant people Israel; that is what they have been chosen for.

Intertextual trajectories. When we expand our view to include intertextual trajectories, we are immediately drawn to the account of the day of Pentecost in Acts 2, which makes explicit reference to the Tower of Babel and manifests the familiar motif of the languages.[22] More specifically we may identify a number of more specific intertextual connections between Acts 2 and Genesis 11–12:

- Luke uses three terms from the LXX of Genesis 11 (v. 4 *glōssais*, tongues; v. 6 *phonēn*, sound; *syncheōmen*, confound).

- The Table of Nations is paralleled in the extensive list of people in attendance in Jerusalem at Pentecost (Acts 2:9).

- After the language confusion is reversed, the covenant is announced as fulfilled ("The promise is for you and your children and for all who are far off" [Acts 2:39]).

On the basis of those explicit connections, we are invited to identify further points of comparison and contrast. The result is that Acts 2 can be seen to serve the function of a canonical-theological inclusio in relationship to Genesis 11–12.

---

[22]Built on observations by John's student Kelly Brady.

Contrasts include the following points:[23]

- The Spirit's descent represents the right establishment of God's presence in Acts 2 contrasted to Yahweh's descent to counteract a flawed initiative in Genesis 11.

- Essence of deity (represented in the Holy Spirit) does not come down to enter the image in the temple (Babylonian model) but to enter his image represented in people, particularly the church—the ultimate expression in New Testament theology of God in the midst of his people.

- With the presence of God rightfully and legitimately established, the differentiation of tongues is symbolically reversed, thus opening universal accessibility to relationship with God.

- Community is disrupted in Genesis, but community is established at Pentecost as God begins regathering his people.

- Pentecost establishes the name of God/Christ through his people rather than establishing their name through what they gain.

- Tower was built to gain unity in divine presence; church is built by God for unity in divine presence.

- In Acts 2 as the people scatter with their own languages to their own homes, they take the presence of God with them rather than leaving a failed project behind.

In conclusion, we can identify some theological implications that may be drawn out given the proposed understanding between Genesis 11–12 and Acts 2.

- Pentecost is seen in New Testament theology as (1) drawing a conclusion to the revelatory program God had initiated in

---

[23]Many of these are identified by M. D. Goulder, *Type and History in Acts* (London: SPCK, 1964), 158-59.

Genesis 12 through the covenant and (2) establishing the new covenant that had been announced in Jeremiah 31.

- The Eden problem is seen in New Testament theology as having been resolved by Christ and reversed in the new creation; the Babel problem is seen as being resolved by the covenant and reversed at Pentecost, where order is brought in the midst of language diversity.

- God's intention through Pentecost is proclaimed by Peter as drawing all nations to himself—a further initiative in divine presence and sacred space reflected in the Pauline theology of believers as a temple.

In the last two propositions, we have considered the accounts of the sons of God and the Tower of Babel, and observed the narrator used recursive narratives (6:1-4; 11:1-9) that characterized their respective antediluvian and postdiluvian eras. Both of these represent the potential restoration of the presence of God (sons of God dwelling among people as a quasi-presence of God; tower building to establish presence of God on earth in the temple). He also used punctuating episodes (fall, flood, tower building) that characterize transitions and should be viewed as actual events, but also may have some archetypal and iterative aspects (repeated human attempts to make themselves the center, recurring floods that brought massive destruction and new beginnings, routine ziggurat building to bring God down). We can now see how these all provide the backstory for the ancestor narratives.

PART 4

THE WORLD:
THINKING ABOUT
EVIDENCE FOR
THE FLOOD

The Flood Story
Has a Real Event Behind It

We do not believe the flood story of the Bible is myth, but neither do we believe the author of Genesis 6–9 intends to give us a straightforward depiction of the event that lies behind it. We believe there is an event that inspired the story; after all, Genesis 6–9 is theological *history*. However, we believe the best understanding of Genesis 1–11, which of course includes the flood account, is that it talks about real events of the past through the use of figurative language. In the case of the flood story, we have identified the use of hyperbole to describe the flood. But there is a real event behind the story just as there was an actual conquest behind the hyperbolic presentation of Joshua's conquest as presented in Joshua 1–12 (see proposition four).

What kind of event would stand behind the flood of Genesis 6–9 (and also other ANE accounts)? We cannot be sure, but we have evidence of more than one flood that would be potential candidates for the inspiration of the story. Again, we are not saying that one of these events is definitely the historical source of the flood stories of the Bible and the ANE. But we are saying there were devastating floods in human prehistory, one of which may well have rooted itself in human memory passed down through the centuries, even millennia, that could have been used as a vehicle by the author of Genesis to present a story that would talk about God's judgment and his restoring order when it had degenerated.

We must be careful here though. In the first place, we need to remember there is absolutely no evidence for a worldwide flood, and there should be if there were such an all-encompassing flood (see proposition fifteen). Second, again, we cannot reconstruct the event, so we don't know for sure whether the story is inspired by a particularly spectacular flood (like the one that took place in what is today Turkey around 5500 BC) or another flood of more normal proportion (though the fact that the precipitating flood lent itself to hyperbole would suggest a flood in the former category). Third, we must be careful not to be dogmatic about evidence for any one flood being the inspiration for the biblical story.

In terms of the third caveat, we think of the cautionary tale provided by the work of Leonard Woolley in the 1920s. Woolley is widely and rightly admired for his important archaeological exploration of Tell al-Muqayyar, which is ancient Ur in southern Mesopotamia. Woolley, who believed in a historical flood, thought that he might uncover evidence of the flood if he dug deeply enough, and sure enough he did under the so-called Royal Cemetery of Ur. He found a layer of silt ten feet thick that had no artifacts in it. He caused quite a stir by claiming that this provided evidence of a massive flood in the alluvial plains of Mesopotamia that, even though local (though thousands of square miles), would seem worldwide. However, comparable flood layers at the same time period were not found in nearby cities, or even throughout the site of Ur itself, and so no one today would agree with Woolley's sensationalist claims.[1] According to Ryan and Pitman, "investigators have determined that the surface area of the

---

[1]For a detailed evaluation of all of the archaeological information sometimes proposed as evidence for a flood in southern Mesopotamia, see Lloyd R. Bailey, *Noah: The Person and the Story in History and Tradition* (Columbia: University of South Carolina, 1989), 28-38.

deposit was localized and perhaps only a single breach in a levee of the Euphrates River, forming what modern hydrologists call a 'splay deposit,' covering at most a few square miles of the lateral floodplain."[2]

While Woolley's flood turned out to be a poor candidate for the one that inspired the biblical (and other ANE) flood stories, we do have evidence of truly momentous floods, any one of which could have so engrained itself in human memory that it would have been passed down from survivors through the generations through oral and ultimately written tradition. This story, based on an actual event, could have been employed by the biblical author to shape an account that served his all-important theological purposes.

One such example that has been suggested is a huge flood that filled a vast desert area to form the Mediterranean Sea. Although this happened over the span of a "single human lifetime" and is of the scale that we are talking about, it must be discarded because it happened five million years ago when there were no human beings to witness it.[3]

As a second example, however, in the past few decades researchers have discovered compelling evidence of a massive flood that could qualify as the type of event that would have fueled the Noah story. The primary researchers were William Ryan and Walter Pitman, both scientists at the Lamont-Doherty Earth Observatory connected to Columbia University. They give an account of their research and their conclusions in a gripping book titled *Noah's Ark: The New Scientific Discoveries About the Event That Changed History*.

While those interested in the evidence may read their book, we here restate their conclusion that a flood "burst through Bosporus in 5600 BC so violently [that it] cleaved Europe from Anatolia."[4] The flood was so overpowering that it turned a freshwater lake into what

---

[2]William Ryan and Walter Pitman, *Noah's Flood: The New Scientific Discoveries About the Event That Changed History* (New York: Simon and Schuster, 1998), 55.
[3]Ibid., 91.
[4]Ibid., 188.

is now the Black Sea. Many who lived on the shores of that no-longer existent freshwater lake and in the general vicinity either were killed or displaced from their homes.

Ryan and Pitman's description of the types of people who experienced this flood is worth the long quotation:

> It seemed quite likely that the humans who were there to witness the Black Sea flood and be driven from their homes by the inundation would have been townspeople, some skilled in tilling fields, planting seeds, harvesting crops, and breeding animals. They may even have been experimenting with the diversion of streams for rudimentary irrigation. Many would have been artisans, bricklayers, carpenters, painters, sculptors, basket weavers, leather workers, jewelers, potters, and morticians. Goods were made for both local consumption and for trade with other distant communities in the Levant and perhaps even in Eastern Europe as Gordon Childe had foreseen. A form of social and political structure would have been in existence, with one class of society conducting administrative tasks, others manual labor, and others such as the shaman performing ceremonies of religion, magic, and even brain surgery. They suffered from diseases including malaria and arthritis. The average human life span was barely thirty years, but a few elders lived into their sixties. One may presume that like their Natufian ancestors thousands of years earlier, when confronted by a drastic change in their environment, they would cope by packing their belongings and departing for a new homeland to carry on with the acquired knowledge, tools, and culture.[5]

Ryan and Pitman suggest that those who survived this flood remembered it as they immigrated to new locations, thus inspiring flood

---

[5]Ibid., 187.

stories that we are aware of among later cultures, including the Babylonian and biblical accounts. We add that each would have taken its specific shape according to the cultural and particularly religious beliefs that they held.

Ryan and Pitman's thesis is intriguing. Before they encountered this evidence, they doubted that the biblical flood story had any reference to a real historical event. Rather, it was pure myth. Now they believe a real event stands behind the flood story.

As intriguing as it is, however, we are not saying this particular flood generated the story of the flood. We do not believe we can reconstruct the historical event from the biblical account. However, we are confident, due to the genre (theological history) of Genesis 6–9 and in our affirmation that the Bible is true in all that it affirms, that there was a historical event. Our conclusion is that the Black Sea flood is the *type* of devastating flood that could have ultimately inspired the biblical account, even if it is not itself the biblical event.[6]

Whatever the precise historical event, the story was told from generation to generation, eventually forming the basis for the *toledot* (or account [see proposition two]) coming down to the Israelite narrators and the later redactors of the final form of the Pentateuch who used the story of Noah and the flood for their important theological message (see proposition eleven).

---

[6]Another theory recently suggested by researchers tries to connect the biblical flood to the incursion of the Persian Gulf into Southern Mesopotamia about eight thousand years ago. The problem with this is that it was not a sudden incursion, but took place over a couple thousand years.

Proposition 15

Geology Does Not Support a Worldwide Flood

Stephen O. Moshier

Any claims about the geographic and hydrological scale of Noah's flood should be testable by observation of the natural world. We typically associate floods with swiftly moving, turbulent water that rises over riverbanks and returns in a period of hours, days, or weeks. But floods also erode surface materials, mostly soil and loose sediment, and deposit them elsewhere. If the Genesis flood covered the entire earth so that every landform was submerged, shouldn't there be significant evidence of erosion and deposition? Indeed, advocates of flood geology make claims for such evidence as promoted in many publications, videos, websites, and popular attractions aimed at an evangelical Christian audience.[1] Yet the worldwide scientific community overwhelmingly rejects the geological interpretations of the flood geologists.[2]

---

[1]Among the most prominent books promoting flood geology include John C. Whitcomb and Henry M. Morris, *The Genesis Flood: The Biblical Record and Its Scientific Implications* (Philadelphia: Presbyterian and Reformed, 1961); Steven A. Austin, *Grand Canyon: Monument to Catastrophe* (El Cajon, CA: Institute for Creation Research, 1994); and Andrew A. Snelling, *Earth's Catastrophic Past: Geology, Creation and the Flood* (Dallas: Institute for Creation Research, 2009).

[2]The mainstream scientific community includes a number of evangelical Christians who do not accept flood geology. Substantial critiques by Christian geologists include Davis A.

What would the world drowned by the flood look like today? A popular advocate of flood geology is fond of saying that we would expect a worldwide flood to deposit "billions of dead things buried in the earth." Indeed, the Renaissance scientists who first studied rocks some four hundred years ago assumed that fossils were evidence of the great biblical deluge. Leonardo da Vinci (1452–1519) compared the disposition of modern beach shells with fossils in rocks and concluded that the fossils had not experienced long-distant, turbulent transport. In subsequent years of research and discovery, natural scientists came to recognize that the biblical flood was not responsible for creating rocks and shaping the landscape.

Geologists developed the concept of the rock cycle from their observations of modern processes and ancient rocks. Field relationships between different kinds of rocks exhibited different kinds of rock formation and recycling: igneous rocks crystallize from magma or lava, sedimentary rocks are composed of particles weathered from older rocks (or, in the case of limestone, from the accumulation of sea shells), and metamorphic rocks transform from older rocks by heat and pressure. Sedimentary rocks provide a historical record of conditions on the earth's surface because they contain evidence of ancient life (fossils and tracks), depositional processes (bedding structures such as ripple marks, mud cracks, raindrop prints, and erosional surfaces), and even past climate conditions (biological and chemical components in the rocks).[3]

The thickness of sedimentary rock varies greatly across the continents and in the ocean basins. There are places on the North American continent, like the Colorado Plateau region, where sedimentary rock layers exceed 25,000 feet in thickness (5 miles or more)! Many of the

Young and Ralph F. Stearley, *The Bible, Rocks and Time: Geological Evidence for the Age of the Earth* (Downers Grove, IL: InterVarsity Press, 2008), and Christian authors contributing chapters in Carol Hill et al., eds., *The Grand Canyon, Monument to an Ancient Earth: Can Noah's Flood Explain the Grand Canyon?* (Grand Rapids: Kregel, 2016).

[3]These features are explained and illustrated for a popular audience in Hill, *Grand Canyon.*

sandstone and shale layers are composed of sand and clay sediment particles that were eroded from rocks exposed in long-disappeared mountain belts. Other layers are composed of limey sediment of shell fragments and mud that accumulated in shallow seas that intermittently covered the continents. The Gulf of Mexico contains over 40,000 feet of sediment that accumulated from sediment shed off of North America and includes 5,000 feet of salt that could form only from evaporation of large volumes of seawater.[4] Based on this kind of global stratigraphic information, the consensus of mainstream geologists for the past 250 years has been that sedimentary rocks preserve records of deposition over hundreds of millions of years.[5]

Flood geologists reinterpret the same global stratigraphic information as evidence supporting a worldwide flood as described in Genesis 7–8. In their scenario, rapidly rising water scoured the preflood landscape and produced sediment particles that were redistributed by swift currents moving beneath the water as it covered the highest mountains. The currents transported vast amounts of sand across continents in a matter of days or months. Indeed, billions of dead things perished and were buried beneath the turbulent waters in thousands of feet of sediment that quickly hardened into sedimentary rock.

How do we test these two opposing views about geology and the flood—"no evidence" versus "it's all evidence"? To the question of What would we expect from a worldwide deluge? we should start by considering exactly what is written in Genesis about the hydrology of the flood. The source of floodwater includes "all the springs of the great deep . . . and the floodgates of the heavens" (Gen 7:11). Rainfall continues for the first 40 of the 150 days when water prevailed (surged) over the earth (Gen 7:12, 24). Water recedes over the next 150 days after a wind passes

---

[4]John M. Armentrout, "Sedimentary Basin Analysis," in *Treatise of Petroleum Geology/Handbook of Petroleum Geology: Exploring for Oil and Gas Traps*, ed. E. A. Beaumont and N. H. Foster (Tulsa: American Association of Petroleum Geologists, 1999), p. 4-1–4-123.

[5]Martin J. S. Rudwick, *Earth's Deep History: How It Was Discovered and Why It Matters* (Chicago: University of Chicago Press, 2014), 360.

over the earth and "the springs of the deep and the floodgates of the heavens had been closed" (Gen 8:1-3). It took an additional 70 days for the land to dry (Gen 8:14). We can estimate how fast the water rose to cover Mount Ararat, which stands 16,854 feet above sea level. Over 150 days water would have to rise an average rate of about 112 feet per day (and the water would have to recede over 150 days at about the same rate).

What can we say about the phenomena described in the narrative? Elsewhere we observed that the narrative reflects an ancient cosmology of subterranean waters beneath a flat earth and waters suspended above the firmament that could be released by opening the gates of heaven. Springs issuing abundant groundwater are common across Mesopotamia and surrounding highlands, owing to the limestone bedrock with complex systems of subterranean fractures (known as karst landscapes). These springs feed the tributaries of the Euphrates and Tigris rivers and are known to swell during seasonal floods.[6] However, a worldwide deluge would require water to flow from the ground and fall from the sky worldwide. There is nothing we know about present earth systems that could explain so much water from rain or groundwater in such short amount of time, so flood geologists argue that the preflood earth was very different from what we observe today. By applying modern geologic concepts not found in the biblical narrative and by going beyond any ANE understanding of the text, they assign the fountains of the great deep to submarine fractures and rifts with water gushing from some vast reservoir in the deep crust or upper mantle.

But just how different was the preflood earth? The narrative lacks specific details about how the landscape changed before and after the flood. There were mountains before the flood. Water covered the mountains. Water drained from the landscape back to the sea. Noah appears to have landed in his own backyard or certainly not far from where the journey began. Yet flood geologists maintain that the entire

[6]Carol A. Hill, "Qualitative Hydrology of Noah's Flood," *Perspectives on Science and Christian Faith* 58 (2006): 120-29.

earth was virtually reshaped during the deluge, and they apply main-stream geological ideas like continental drift and plate tectonics to their scenarios. Ignoring physical constraints and mechanical properties of the earth's crust, they envision lithospheric plates moving as fast as 5-10 miles per day (currently plates move at rates of inches per year). Curiously, flood geologists avoid appealing to miraculous intervention from God in the course of physical processes during the deluge.

A leading organization promoting a global flood proposes five categories of geological evidence. In general presentation, the evidence seems intuitively reasonable. However, on careful analysis, each claim misrepresents what is actually known about the geology.

1. Seashell fossils in rocks above sea level. Flood geologists ask how sedimentary rocks containing abundant remains of marine fossils could have been deposited thousands of feet above sea level unless ocean water flooded the continents. Yet there are many places on earth today where very thick deposits of sediment and sedimentary rock are accumulating on continental crust below sea level.[7] As layer-upon-layer of sediment deposits, the layers compact and the underlying crust depresses like stacking heavy books on a flimsy mattress. These processes allow many miles of sediment to accumulate in a body of water that maintains fairly constant depth (a good example is the modern Gulf of Mexico). Tectonic activity can cause the continental crust containing the layers of sedimentary rock to push upward above sea level. Fossil-bearing rocks in mountain belts were deformed (faulted and folded) during past episodes of crustal uplift. Places like the Colorado Plateau experienced broad up-warping of the crust without extensive deformation (as a flat board can warp if it takes on moisture).

---

[7]Examples include all of the wide continental shelves surrounding the Atlantic Ocean and Gulf of Mexico, the North Sea between the United Kingdom and Norway, the Gulf of Carpenteria between Australia and Papua/Papua New Guinea, and the South China Sea, to name a few.

2. **Rock layers over entire continents.** Geologists designate different sedimentary rock layers into distinct formations that can be traced laterally over great distances across the continent. Flood geologists reason that only a global flood could transport sediment across the continents.[8] Many sedimentary rock layers cover vast areas of the continents, but no single layer covers an entire continent from one end to the other as flood geologists claim. In fact, detailed mapping shows that rock layers overlap one another like leaves piled up on a lawn. Rather than finding evidence of one massive deluge, mainstream geologists find abundant evidence of multiple periods of rising and falling sea level that changed by as much as four hundred feet higher or lower than at present.[9] It's the combination of low-standing continental crust (see point 1) and high-standing sea level, followed by uplift, that results in these sedimentary layers existing now above sea level.

3. **Rapid deposition of sand carried across continents.** The deposition of sand across continents pertains to flood geologists' study of one particular rock formation in the Grand Canyon, the Coconino Sandstone. Mainstream geologists interpret bedding structures and small animal tracks in the rock layers as representing an ancient sand dune desert environment. The unit is up to 600 feet thick in the Grand Canyon and 1,000 feet thick to the south in Arizona. Sand particles appear to have been transported by rivers to the place of deposition from a source of older bedrock some 600 miles to the west and north (in present-day Utah and Wyoming). Having desert rock deposited in the middle of the flood is a problem for flood geology, so flood geologists interpret the sand to have been transported by swift currents

---

[8]In fact, major river systems move sediment vast distances across continents involving local floods. But contemplate how long it might take for a grain of sand from Minnesota to reach the Mississippi River Delta (decades, centuries, millennia?).

[9]Kenneth G. Miller et al., "The Phanerozoic Record of Global Sea-Level Change," *Science* 310 (2005): 1293-98.

of two to four miles per hour, under deep water.[10] To fit in the flood-year time frame, the Coconino Formation would have to have been deposited in a matter of days, requiring a mass of sand hundreds of feet thick and hundreds of miles wide to be moving at several miles per hour across thousands of square miles![11] This catastrophic-deposition scenario does not adequately explain how dainty animal tracks could be abundantly preserved in the bedding.

Consider the fabulous rates of deposition that are required to deposit over 25,000 feet of sediment in one region of the earth or 40,000 feet in another. If deposition occurred over 150 to 200 days, that would mean throwing down some 150 to 200 feet of sediment on the sea floor per day! A widespread flood geology view is that the strata exposed in the Grand Canyon represent early flood deposition over the period of the first 150 days of the flood year. Hence, about 4,000 feet of sediment would have been deposited there at an average rate of about twenty-seven feet per day or about one foot per hour.[12]

4. Layers made in rapid succession. Another problem is the thick series of sedimentary rock layers that are folded with bends in the strata of as much as 90 degrees. Because they do not observe evidence of brittle fracture in the layers, flood geologists claim that bending occurred after the layers accumulated in rapid succession but before the sediment hardened into solid rock.[13] In fact, mainstream geologists have reported on abundant evidence of brittle fracture and slippage along surfaces between layers in these rocks.[14] This kind of deformation

---

[10]Andrew A. Snelling, "Sand Transported Cross Country: Flood Evidence Number Four," *Answers* 3, no. 4 (2008): 96-99.

[11]Timothy K. Helble, "Sediment Transport and the Coconino Sandstone: A Reality Check on Flood Geology," *Perspectives on Science and the Christian Faith* 63, no. 1 (2011): 25-41.

[12]Ibid.

[13]Snelling, *Earth's Catastrophic Past*, 599-601.

[14]Louis Cyril Niglio, "Fracture Analysis of Precambrian and Paleozoic Rocks in Selected Areas of the Grand Canyon National Park, USA" (master's thesis, University of Oklahoma, Norman, 2004), 68.

can occur in hard rock if high levels of stress are applied to the rock over long periods of time.

5. No slow and gradual erosion. There should be no evidence of erosion or exposure to air between or within sedimentary rock layers if they were deposited in rapid succession beneath the flood-water. However, contacts showing evidence for erosion or nondeposition between layers in successions of sedimentary rock, called *unconformities*, are common on every continent. Flood geologists cite "knife edge" contacts between formations in the Grand Canyon as evidence of continuous and uninterrupted sedimentation from top to bottom of the rock sequence. They recognize only one major unconformity in the Grand Canyon sequence, known as the Great Unconformity, representing the beginning of flood deposition. However, there are at least *nineteen* documented unconformities in the 5,000-foot sequence of sedimentary rock in the Grand Canyon! Two such formation contacts feature spectacular buried channels that formed after the underlying units were deposited and their upper surfaces were eroded. Later, the channels were filled with sediment from the overlying formation. Mainstream geologists consider this as evidence of long-term sea level rise and fall across the continents (much the way sea level rose and fell hundred of meters several times over the past two million years during the Ice Age). One of those formations exhibiting erosion on its upper surface is the Redwall Limestone. Along with the channels, we find ancient sinkholes and caves that eventually collapsed or were filled with sediment from the overlying formation.[15] Caves form in solid limestone as fresh groundwater dissolves the soluble rock over thousands of years. Evidence of unconformities and ancient caves negates the flood geology interpretation of rapid deposition with no slow or gradual erosion.

---

[15]George H. Billingsley and Stanley S. Beus, "Geology of the Surprise Canyon Formation of the Grand Canyon, Arizona," *Museum of Northern Arizona Bulletin* 61 (1999): 254.

A rather serious problem for flood geology involves explaining the abundance and distribution of some of the common types of sedimentary rock (e.g., the thick salt deposits in the Gulf of Mexico). Shale is the most abundant sedimentary rock on earth (greater than 50 percent). Clay minerals that compose shale and other mudrocks are derived from the chemical weathering of minerals, including feldspar and mica that are abundant in older igneous rocks. In contrast, the mineral quartz, which is the predominant mineral in sandstone and siltstone, is not altered during chemical weathering. Clay accumulates in the soil cover over bedrock. Soil erosion removes the clay by wind and water transport to lakes or to the sea, where clay settles out of suspension in calm water conditions (turbulence keeps the clay in suspension). All the clay in the most abundant rock in the earth's crust had to be created through soil formation before it could be deposited. All the soil on earth at any given moment in its history could not provide enough clay for all of these rocks! The turbulence of the rising and falling floodwaters, so often touted by flood geologists, would tend to keep clay particles in permanent suspension!

Limestone is composed of whole shells, broken shells, and limey mud. The shells in limestone have not been transported far from where the animals and calcareous algae lived on the sea floor. Most of the types of ancient limestone can be compared to deposits on modern coastlines, like on the Bahamas Platform, Florida Bay, the Persian Gulf, and the Great Barrier Reef. They form in shallow water below the tides and on intertidal mud flats. All the seashell animals on earth at any given moment in its history could not provide enough limey sediment for the total thickness of limestone around the world! Limey sediment could not have been derived from the erosion of older limestone rocks by advancing floodwater, either. Remember the caves and sinkholes? Because limestone is so soft and soluble, weathering limestone does not produce much sediment.

We began this proposition with the question, If the Genesis flood covered the entire earth so that every landform was submerged, shouldn't there be significant evidence of erosion and deposition? Since the global sedimentary rock record is inconsistent with a worldwide flood, what kind of evidence might be more favorable to such a deluge? That is hard to say because it's extremely difficult to consider what physical processes might have accompanied a worldwide flood. An event of such magnitude has never been observed in the modern era of scientific investigation. The best we can do is "scale up" from the most catastrophic observable processes that occur more locally. For example, the recent devastating tsunamis that ravaged the Indian Ocean (2004) and Japan (2011) give us some clues about rapidly rising water across large distances. Tsunami waves as high as 30 meters above normal seawater advancing several kilometers landward and speeds of 10-20 miles per hour can easily destroy humanmade structures. However, geologists have discovered that tsunami sediment deposits are generally less than 25 centimeters (10 inches) thick and conform to the antecedent landscape (that is, no significant change in topography).[16] Large coastal storms also surge water landward of the coast, but storm deposits are only slightly thicker and confined to the beach and near shore.

We estimated that to flood the earth to the highest mountains in 150 days would require water to rise just over 100 feet per day (and fall at about the same rate). While this sounds like a dramatic rise, especially to any living soul not in the ark, it's possible that not all that much sediment would be produced or moved very far during the advance or fall. Most of the geological work of erosion would occur at the water-land interface (the rising shoreline), but just as with a surging tsunami there is not much time to excavate large quantities of sediment. Furthermore, at 10 miles per hour for a typical tsunami

---

[16]Robert A. Morton, Guy Gelfenbaum, and Bruce E. Jaffe, "Physical Criteria for Distinguishing Sandy Tsunami and Storm Deposits Using Modern Examples," *Sedimentary Geology* 200 (2007): 184-207.

(which equals 126,720 feet per day), that's some 1,130 times faster than our estimate for the rising or falling global floodwater! A rate of 100 feet per day is far too slow to move even grains of sand![17]

The impact of rising floodwater over the earth's surface can be illustrated on a hypsometric curve, a graph showing the percentage of the land surface and ocean floor at different elevations and depths (see fig. 1). As the floodwater begins to rise above sea level, it would cross lower elevations that represent about 20 percent of the earth's total surface area or about 70 percent of the earth's total land surface area. Despite the large surface area, the lower elevation would not provide much erosional potential. With the previously discussed rates of water rise, erosion would be limited to surface material with hard bedrock left largely untouched. Only 10 percent of the earth's total surface area or about 30 percent of the earth's total land surface area lies above the average land elevation. The upland surface area would produce less sediment, but certainly there is more erosional potential with steeper slopes. It's likely that some of the sediment produced at higher elevations would be swept to lower elevations (but not far offshore from normal sea level). During the 150-day period of water recession, more sediment may be eroded and transported to lower elevations, but again, the velocity of the receding floodwater is not too effective to erode or move sediment.[18] The significance of this exercise is that nothing like the tens of thousands of feet of sediment and sedimentary rock found in different places around the globe would be generated during a one-year, worldwide flood.[19]

---

[17]One hundred feet/day equates to 0.04 cm/sec. Based on experimental and field observations of sediment particle movement, current velocities of 10 to 100 cm/sec are required to move sand particles (sand size ranges from 1/16 mm to 2 mm in diameter).

[18]Other submarine processes could be involved in the redistribution of sediment other than erosion by rising and falling floodwater. Flood geologists advocate submarine landslides and gravity currents (turbidity flows) for some rock layers in the Grand Canyon. However, the exercise here shows that there would not be too much sediment to redistribute.

[19]A flood geologist might respond that the hypsometric profile of the preflood world may have been different and that tectonic upheavals might have raised and lowered landmasses during the flood (earlier, we mentioned rapid plate tectonics). Yet mountains supposedly raised during the flood very often contain the hard sedimentary rocks claimed to have been

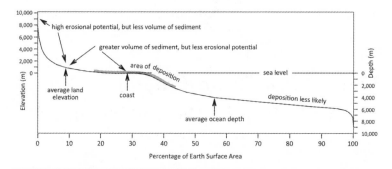

Figure 1. A hypsometric curve applied to the potential for rising and falling global floodwater to create and distribute sediment. The rate of water rise and fall, following the biblical narrative, would not produce the volume of sedimentary rock we see distributed around the world.

Is there geological evidence for a worldwide flood? The science of geology started with this question as a primary objective. The early generations of geologists, especially by the middle of the nineteenth century, determined that thick successions of sedimentary rocks they studied were not deposited in the flood of Noah. Rather, they concluded that the rocks were deposited over vast periods of *deep time* by processes generally observable on the modern earth. Contemporary geologists share that view with an even more extensive knowledge of earth's history and dynamic structure. Flood geology is a project to reinterpret the rock record to conform to a highly elaborated interpretation of the flood narrative in Genesis. Flood geology is motivated solely on the belief that the Bible demands a worldwide flood. Proponents appeal to speculative assumptions about geological processes accompanying the flood that are neither mentioned in the narrative nor evident in nature. We do not find that the biblical narrative requires a worldwide flood, nor do we find geological evidence of it in any particular ancient rock formation or feature of the modern landscape.

deposited by the flood (da Vinci observed this 500 years ago)! Rising and falling land-masses beneath the deluge would not result in the massive formation and distribution of sedimentary rock that we observe today. This is only one way among many that global flood interpretations are internally inconsistent.

Flood Stories from Around the World Do Not Prove a Worldwide Flood

Perhaps you have been told there are flood stories from many places around the world, and that is true.[1] But perhaps that information has been used to suggest to you that such flood stories prove that there was a worldwide flood, and that is false.

There are many flood stories from around the world, but mostly from places with a high probability and experience of frequent floods. Some people use this as an argument that all of these stories go back to a worldwide flood and were passed down in the following genera- tions as people spread through the world, carrying with them the ac- count that ultimately goes back to Noah and his three sons, which one reading of the story would understand to be the ancestors of everyone who is alive today. Thus, the existence of flood stories in America, Australia, the Pacific Islands, Europe (ancient Greece and then

---

[1] An early modern collection of these flood stories may be found in J. G. Fraser, *Folk-Lore in the Old Testament: Studies in Comparative Religion, Legend, and Law* (1918; repr., New York: Macmillan, 1927), 46-143. See also T. H. Gaster, *Myth, Legend, and Custom in the Old Testa- ment* (New York: Harper Torchbooks, 1969), 82-131. Analysis in Lloyd R. Bailey, *Noah: The Person and the Story in History and Tradition* (Columbia: University of South Carolina Press, 1989), 5-10.

medieval stories, but not many), Africa (not many), and Asia (not many) would attest to a worldwide flood.

This argument is roughly the one made by Charles Martin in his popular book *Flood Legends: Global Clues of a Common Event.*[2] He believes myths have events behind them. He then points out that there are many flood myths from around the world, and introduces the concept of "telephone mythology," the name deriving from the popular game of "telephone." In telephone, someone speaks a statement into the ear of one person, who turns around and tells it to another person, and on and on. The message gets passed down, but in the process it also changes, except for maybe the big idea. This process informs his understanding of how the many flood stories developed over time as peoples descended from Noah and his three sons, split into different people groups, and then developed their own cultures and religions, which shaped how they told the story. Even so, he argues the basic idea of a great flood persists in these various stories. In particular, he compares the flood story in the *Mahabharata* (India [Hindu]), the story among the Karina (Carib Indians in eastern Venezuela), and Genesis. Rather than critique his comparison of these three flood legends, we rather will raise some questions about the whole approach.

In a word, Martin and others like him do not make a very compelling argument. First, the fact that there are flood stories from different parts of the world does not mean it was experienced in these parts; rather, the argument goes, it was passed down from the time of the flood. In other words, the flood legends would not be an argument to support a worldwide flood over, say, a local flood.

A more reasonable explanation for the pervasiveness of flood stories around the world is that a catastrophic but local flood so impressed people that it was handed down and across cultures as a

---

[2]Charles Martin, *Flood Legends: Global Clues of a Common Event* (Green Forest, AR: Master Books, 2009).

worldwide flood story. Indeed, if our view is correct—that the Bible's (rhetorically) worldwide flood has a catastrophic local flood behind it—then it well could have made such an impression on various peoples that it was shared more broadly by ripple effect.

Second, with the obvious exception of the ancient Near Eastern flood stories we studied in proposition seven, and perhaps the Greek flood story (that may have been influenced by the same experience or influenced by the ancient Near Eastern account),[3] there is only the most superficial connection between most of these flood stories, mainly that there was a flood with survivors. It is much more likely that many flood stories emerged in different cultures based on their own experience of floods. As one scholar says,

> We know . . . that numerous peoples have no flood legend in their literature. Flood stories are almost entirely lacking in Africa, occur only occasionally in Europe, and are absent in many parts of Asia. They are widespread in America, Australia, and the islands of the Pacific. In addition, many of the known flood legends differ radically from the biblical story and stand independent of it and of one another. Many do not know a world-wide flood at all, but only a local inundation; not all relate the rescue of a man or a family who "found favor in the eyes of the Lord." Often the heroes save themselves in boats or by scaling mountains, without intervention of the gods. Further, only a few of the flood stories give the wickedness of man as the cause of the Flood. In many instances nothing can be said about either the characteristics of the Flood or the means of its origin. Often storms cause an inundation, some-times rains and ocean tidal waves, occasionally earthquakes. The saved may be a single person (man or woman), a couple,

---

[3]See M. Astour, *Hellenosemitica: An Ethnic and Cultural Study in West Semitic Impact on Mycenaean Greece* (Leiden: Brill, 1967).

an entire family, a definite or an indefinite number of people. Only in a few sagas are seeds and representatives of various species of animals taken into the vessel of deliverance. The duration of the Flood, if given, varies from a few days to many years.[4]

Third, many of the most similar flood stories, like the medieval European ones and the American Indian ones, were likely influenced by the biblical story itself. As missionaries told the story of the biblical flood to the native inhabitants of North America, some biblical ideas could have gotten fused to some native Indian ones.

Thus it seems to us to be wrongminded to put any stock in the argument that the existence of flood legends from around the world offers any support to the idea that there was a worldwide flood. In essence, these stories are irrelevant for our understanding of the biblical account.

EXCURSUS: MODERN QUESTS
FOR NOAH'S ARK ARE ILL-FOUNDED

This topic has been treated in detail in Lloyd Bailey's thorough and judiciously balanced evaluation. Readers can find all the detail that they want there, so we will only quote his conclusion:

Research into this type of evidence for the ark's survival is . . . fraught with difficulties. The sources are often third- and fourth-hand. Years could be and have been spent in trying to verify some of them. The original documents often cannot be found—if in fact they ever existed. Alleged eyewitnesses have died and thus cannot verify reports attributed to them, or clarify critical details. The reports are filled with discrepancies, some minor but others so substantial as to raise the question of

---

[4]J. H. Marks, "Flood," *IDB* 2:280.

credibility. A few are expressed in such strident, polemical tones as to destroy any claim of objectivity. Without questioning the integrity of some reporters, it appears that details have been added as their observations were retold.[5]

---

[5]Bailey, *Noah*, 88, cited in Walton, *Genesis*, 321.

Science Can Purify Our Religion; Religion Can Purify Science from Idolatry and False Absolutes

We recognize that some readers might be troubled if it seems to them that we are taking our cues from modern science. "Doesn't Scripture trump science?" they may ask. After all, the Bible is God's Word to humanity and therefore always true. Science is a human endeavor and thus susceptible to all the errors and faults of humanity.

We have already asserted our affirmation of the view that the Bible is indeed inerrant in all that it intends to teach. We also agree that any human project is subject to miscalculation and error. But to pit the Bible against science in this fashion is problematic for more than one reason.

First, orthodox Christianity has traditionally affirmed a "two book" view of God's truth. God reveals himself in both the Bible and in nature. Such a two-book approach to truth is well expressed in the classic Reformed Belgic Confession:

This chapter title is adapted from a quotation by John Paul II: "Science can purify religion from error and superstition; religion can purify science from idolatry and false absolutes." "To the Reverend George V. Coyne SJ, Director of the Vatican Observatory," June 1, 1988, http://w2.vatican.va/content/john-paul-ii/en/letters/1988/documents/hf_jp-ii_let _19880601_padre-coyne.html.

We know him by two means; first, by the creation, preservation and government of the universe; which is before our eyes as a most elegant book, wherein all creatures, great and small, are as so many characters leading us to contemplate the invisible things of God, namely His power and divinity, as the apostle Paul says, Rom. 1:20. All which things are sufficient to convince men, and leave them without excuse. Secondly, he makes himself more clearly fully known to us by his holy and divine Word, that is to say, as far as is necessary for us to know in this life, to his glory and our salvation.[1]

This insightful comment leads theologians to distinguish between general revelation, directed to all people, and special revelation that comes through Scripture, which is necessary for salvation. But general revelation also reveals truth to us, and since both books are ultimately "written" by God, they will not ultimately conflict if properly understood, the latter provision applying as much to scriptural interpretation as it does to our understanding of nature.

The reason we should not be afraid to study nature through scientific means is that, since it reflects God's truth, it will never contradict the Bible when both are rightly understood, and that leads to our next point.

Second, we have to remember that our understanding of both science and Scripture are the result of interpretation. We understand and must take into consideration that our scientific interpretations of nature may well be incorrect. It is legitimate to question scientific conclusions, though we must be careful not to manipulate the evidence or appeal to miracle when there is no reason to think God acted in such a way or to suggest that conditions were different in the distant past without evidence that they were.[2]

---

[1] The Belgic Confession, article 2, found at www.creeds.net/belgic.
[2] Unfortunately, these strategies are often employed by those who try to undermine the findings of mainstream science in an attempt to defend their own interpretation of Scripture.

What Christians often forget, however, is that while the Bible is true in all that it intends to teach, our interpretations are not always correct. We need to be open to the possibility that we have wrongly understood a particular passage, perhaps not completely but in some important way.

Before proceeding with illustrations as well as talking about how science can assist us in our interpretation, we need to pause here to state our agreement with those who insist on the perspicuity (clarity) of Scripture. We must be open to changing our interpretation, both as individuals and as a church. Further, we are often given greater clarity about the meaning of a passage by something external to the Scriptures themselves.

Since the Reformation, the Protestant church has correctly and vigorously defended the perspicuity and sufficiency of Scripture. *Perspicuity* is a technical term for clarity, and the Bible *is* clear. Unfortunately, some readers take this to mean that the Bible is clear in everything that it says. But that is not the case. The following statement from the Westminster Confession of Faith illustrates the doctrine:

> All things in Scripture are not alike plain in themselves, nor alike clear unto all: yet those things which are necessary to be known, believed, and observed for salvation, are so clearly propounded, and opened in some place of Scripture or other, that not only the learned, but the unlearned, in a due use of the ordinary means, may attain unto a sufficient understanding of them. (WCF 1.7)

Though the Hebrew and Greek (and a smattering of Aramaic) have to be translated, when it comes to the important main message of the Bible ("those things which are necessary to be known, believed, and observed for salvation"), these things "are so clearly propounded, and opened in some place of Scripture or other" that not even a bad translator could mess it up.

See, for example, K. Ham's contribution in *Four Views on Creation, Evolution, and Intelligent Design*, ed. J. B. Stump (Grand Rapids: Zondervan, 2017).

But what is necessary to know for salvation?

Well, that would be "I am a sinner, and I need help. Jesus died and was raised to save me from sin and death, and I must put my faith in him."

Yes, pretty basic. And so clearly taught in Scripture we must work hard to miss the point.

This is the gospel, and it fits in with the big story of the Bible, which we also think is clear:

Creation—Fall (into Sin)—Redemption—Consummation

This is the basic plot of the Bible from Genesis to Revelation. God created all things, including human beings, whom he created morally innocent. Humans chose to rebel against God, thus explaining the presence of sin and death. God then pursued reconciliation by redeeming his human creatures from their sin. (This is the main point of the bulk of the Bible, Genesis 4 through Revelation 20.) The biblical account ends with a description of the future consummation (the New Jerusalem [Rev 21–22]). Denying this big picture presented by the Bible is indeed problematic.

But, as the confession states (and notice the statement leads with this), "All things in Scripture are not alike plain in themselves, nor alike clear unto all." Not all things are clear in Scripture. We need to remember that when we interact with people with opinions different from ours on subjects not essential for our salvation.

When it comes to one's view on the flood—is it worldwide or local or, as argued in this book, is it using hyperbole to picture a local flood as a worldwide flood to communicate a theological message?—we are not dealing with the heart of the gospel. No wonder we have disagreements among us. The doctrine of perspicuity is not under threat by our different interpretations.

The doctrine of the sufficiency of Scripture is based on the Reformation principle of *sola Scriptura*. The Bible is all we need in order to understand our need for salvation and the means of that salvation. We don't need extrabiblical resources (ancient Near Eastern texts, scientific insights, archaeological discoveries, etc.) to know we are sinners and Christ died for our sins and was raised in glory.

That said, the doctrine of the sufficiency of Scripture does not deny that we can be greatly helped in our desire to know the original meaning of biblical texts with these extrabiblical recourses, and that is our point in this book. We are helped in our attempt to understand the author's intended meaning in the flood story by both ancient Near Eastern accounts of the flood and also scientific conclusions related to the possibility of a worldwide deluge.

We have many examples of dramatic changes in the church's interpretation of Scriptures in the light of evidence from outside the Bible. We give two examples before returning to the topic of the flood.

The first example concerns the Song of Songs. Today the vast consensus, especially among Protestant interpreters, is that the Song is love poetry. There is disagreement over whether it is a poem that tells a story about two or three characters, or is an anthology of love poems, but virtually everyone reads it as love poetry.[3]

But that was not the case before the nineteenth century. Before that time both the church and the synagogue considered the Song an allegory of the relationship between God and his people, the church among the former and Israel among the latter. Thus, among Jewish interpreters it was typical to take Song of Songs 1:2-4 not as an expression of desire for intimacy on the part of the woman for her beloved, but as a reference to the exodus from Egypt:

Let him kiss me with the kisses of his mouth—
    for your love is more delightful than wine.
Pleasing is the fragrance of your perfumes;

---

[3]For details, see Tremper Longman III, *Song of Songs*, NICOT (Grand Rapids: Eerdmans, 2001), 20-49.

> your name is like perfume poured out.
> No wonder the young women love you!
>   Take me away with you—let us hurry!
> Let the king bring me into his chambers.

After all, if the Song is an allegory where the woman represents Israel and the man represents God, then it makes sense to read this as Israel (the woman) asking God (the man) to bring it into Israel (his chambers). But what happened in the nineteenth century to convince readers that the Song was love poetry, not an allegory? More than one factor to be sure, but a key one was the rediscovery of Egyptian and ancient Near Eastern love poetry.[4] Something outside of Scripture helped modern readers understand the ancient meaning of the Song of Songs better than it was understood during the medieval and even the Reformation period.

Our second example is closer to the subject at hand, being an example where new insights in science changed our reading of a biblical text. In other words, here we have an example of "science refining theology."

In the early church and during the medieval period, it was thought that the Bible taught that the earth was the center of the solar system. After all, the sun rose and the sun set. In Joshua 10, God stopped the sun in the sky. This and other language suggested to readers that the Bible taught that the earth was the center of the solar system.

Into the context of such belief stepped astronomer Galileo (1564–1642). His story is well known, though occasionally exaggerated. Without giving the history that led up to his discovery, suffice it to say that he more than ruffled ecclesiastical feathers by asserting that his observations confirmed that the earth was not the center of the universe or even the solar system.[5]

---

[4]For a full account, see ibid., 49-54.

[5]Kerry Magruder, "Galilei, Galileo," in *The Dictionary of Christianity and Science*, ed. Paul Copan et al. (Grand Rapids: Zondervan, 2017), 298-300.

The church reacted to his pronouncements suggesting that he was a heretic for undermining the clear teaching of Scripture. Today, virtually everyone, even the most conservative, not only agrees with Galileo's perspective about the universe but finds it difficult to believe his views were thought to be a threat to biblical truth and the Christian religion.

The lesson we should derive from these examples, particularly the Galileo incident, is that the church should not respond with a knee-jerk negative reaction to scientific discoveries that appear to question our interpretation of the Bible. If they are accurate descriptions of reality, they are not going to conflict with the Bible. Rather, our reaction should be to go back to Scripture and see if we understood the text correctly or whether there might be a better reading in the sense that it takes us back to the intention of the author.

We should take Augustine's admonition, worth quoting at length, to heart:

Usually even a non-Christian knows something about the earth, the heavens, and the other elements of this world, about the motion and orbit of the stars and even their size and relative positions, about the predictable eclipses of the sun and moon, the cycles of the years and the seasons, about the kinds of animals, shrubs, stones, and so forth, and this knowledge he holds to as being certain from reason and experience. Now, it is a disgraceful and dangerous thing for an infidel to hear a Christian, presumably giving the meaning of Holy Scripture, talking nonsense on these topics, and we should take all means to prevent such an embarrassing situation, in which people show up vast ignorance in a Christian and laugh it to scorn. The shame is not so much that an ignorant individual is derided, but that people outside the household of faith think our sacred writers held such opinions, and, to the great loss for whose salvation we toil, the writers of our Scriptures are criticized and rejected as unlearned men. If they find a Christian mistaken in a field which they themselves know well and hear him maintaining his foolish opinions about our books, how are they going to believe those books in matters concerning the resurrection of the dead, the hope of eternal life, and the kingdom of heaven, when they think their pages are full of falsehoods and on facts which they themselves have learnt from experience and the light of reason? Reckless and incompetent expounders of Holy Scripture bring untold trouble and sorrow on their wiser brethren when they are caught in one of their mischievous false opinions and are taken to task by those who are not bound by the authority of our sacred books.[6]

But does this work in the other direction? How does religion "purify science"?

We certainly believe it does, but perhaps not in precisely the same way as science informs religion. The reason for this is that the Bible does not intend to teach us scientific truth. While not impossible, we don't think the Bible will disqualify legitimate scientific conclusions. Most importantly, we don't think Christians should make pronouncements about what they can research and what may or may not be discovered. For instance, we should not discourage scientists from seeing whether they can discover a scientific basis for the origin of life. If God created the first organic material by a special act of creation, then a scientific explanation will not be forthcoming. But it is possible that God used secondary causes to bring forth life, just as many believe he used secondary causes to bring into existence the first humans. That God's actions can be explained by providence rather than miracle

---

[6]Augustine, *Literal Meaning of Genesis* 5.11, 162, quoted in Conor Cunningham, *Darwin's Pious Idea: Why the Ultra-Darwinists and Creationists Both Get It Wrong* (Grand Rapids: Eerdmans, 2010), 294.

does not make it any less God's action. The Bible is more interested in affirming his agency in creation, not the mechanisms that were used.

Religion informing science, we would argue, goes back to the foundations of science. Science operates on biblical foundations that understand there are consistencies in the cosmos. God created an ordered cosmos that can be studied by observation, and he gave his human creatures intelligence so they can come to certain conclusions based on their observations. Thus, we may not be surprised when the historian of science Ted Davis reports, "Nevertheless, even if the Scientific Revolution was not an inherently Christian phenomenon, it was carried out almost entirely by Christians."[7]

Second, religion must challenge science when it oversteps its bounds and proclaims itself the sole arbiter of truth, particularly when scientists start proclaiming in the name of science that religion is false. Here is where science becomes idolatry, and unfortunately, while the great majority of scientists know better, there are a handful of well-known exceptions. Perhaps the best-known today include Richard Dawkins and Stephen Hawking, both eminent scientists, who demonstrate their ignorance when they speak about religion, embarrassing even many nonreligious scientists and intellectuals.[8]

It is disheartening, therefore, to see how some Christians, including Christian leaders, treat science as some sort of enemy of the faith. Such an attitude results in all kinds of damage. First, it damages the reputation of the Bible and the church since it requires people not only to question some of the conclusions scientists reach but also, when the

---

[7]See Edward B. Davis, "Scientific Revolution," in *Dictionary of Christianity and Science*, ed. Paul Copan et al. (Grand Rapids: Zondervan, 2017), 619-21. See also Edward B. Davis, "Christianity and Early Modern Science: The Foster Thesis Reconsidered," in *Evangelicals and Science in Historical Perspective*, ed. David N. Livingstone, D. G. Hart, and Mark A. Noll (Oxford: Oxford University Press, 1999), 75-95.

[8]See for instance, Richard Dawkins, *The God Delusion* (repr., New York: Mariner Books, 2008); and Stephen Hawking and Leonard Mlodinow, *The Grand Design* (New York: Bantam Books, 2012). See also Terry Eagleton, review of *The God Delusion*, by Richard Dawkins, *The London Review of Books* 28 (2006): 32-34.

evidence is overwhelming—for instance, in the case of the flood—to try to undermine the very foundation of science. This move is particularly perplexing since the foundation of science is compatible with, if not inspired, by the biblical worldview.

Thus, rather than shrinking from the charge that science has caused us to go back to the biblical account of the flood to see if we are reading it correctly, we fully embrace it since it has led us to read the account in conformity with the author's intention.

Conclusion

Methodologically, we have noted that events are not authoritative; *interpretation* of events by the biblical authors is what carries authority. Of course, for the interpretation to be authoritative, there must be an event behind the interpretation (see proposition fourteen). However, the reality of the event is not found in its reconstruction but in the literary and theological place the author gives it. Events themselves are viewed differently in the ancient world, and any recounting is inevitably shaped by their literary conventions, theological assumptions and objectives, and cultural perspectives. This is especially true of events carrying cosmic significance. The biblical author is not authoritatively describing an event (in a way that would prove its historical authenticity to the satisfaction of a skeptic) but is authoritatively interpreting what God was doing through the event using his own perceptions and conventions. Authority therefore does not depend on our ability to reconstruct the extent of the event or to defend scientifically whatever reconstruction we might offer.

We have noted the importance of recognizing the use of rhetorical devices to shape the narrative so we can discern how the narrative of Genesis 6–9 is working. Since Genesis is a literary representation that has been constructed rhetorically to achieve theological purposes, we should not expect to be able to use it to reconstruct the (real) event. As an illustration, we would not expect to be able to look at Van Gogh's *Starry Night* in order to reconstruct aspects such as which part of the sky it shows, which hemisphere, and what time of night, and match it to a shot from the Hubble telescope. Though the starry sky is real, Van Gogh offers an artistic representation. Literary descriptions are likewise artistic. In a similar way, then, we would not expect to be able to take a rhetorically shaped account of an ancient flood tradition and reconstruct it in modern hydrological-geological terms. Our inability to do so is not because it is false but because it is culturally situated literary art using rhetorical conventions.

The rhetoric we recognize from the ancient Near East depicts the scope and effect in cosmic proportions.[1] We can classify the flood narrative as a "cataclysm account" and then identify cataclysm accounts in the ANE and the Bible as being characterized in cosmic proportions. This same characterization was noted as also found in another genre, apocalyptic. As such it uses hyperbole as part of a universalistic rhetoric shown to be part of the repertoire of biblical authors in other places in Scripture.

In the literary development of Genesis 1–11, the author/compiler interprets the flood as parallel to creation, which was an order-bringing event, but is also parallel to the covenant, which stands as a strategy to extend order. In the theological development the account provides yet another example of sin and judgment, illustrating how God responds to sin in dramatic ways yet continues to carry out his plans and purposes.

We have developed the idea that Genesis 1–11 in general, and the flood narrative within it, provides the backstory for the covenant with Abraham and his family that unfolds in the ancestor narratives in Genesis 12–50. God extends grace to humanity through the covenant, he brings order through the Torah within the covenant, and he continues to move toward the restoration of his presence on earth, lost at Eden and reestablished in the tabernacle.

---

[1]Yi Samuel Chen, *The Primeval Flood Catastrophe* (Oxford: Oxford University Press, 2013), 204.

Consequently, if we were to pose the question, Why does the compiler of Genesis include Genesis 1–11? the answer would not be that he wanted us to know about these events. Rather, he is using these well-known events of the past to help the reader understand how the covenant with Abraham fits into the flow of God's plans and purposes for the cosmos, for his creatures, for his people, and for history. The backstory of Genesis 1–11 explains how and why God came to identify a particular people he chose to be in covenant relationship with.

We have noted that even though the biblical account is developed along the same conversational lines as the Mesopotamian accounts, the interpretation of the account in Genesis is dramatically different from what we find in Mesopotamian tradition. It is clear they are in dialogue in the same cultural river, but Genesis takes a radical departure from the interpretation that emerges from the literature of Mesopotamia.

Turning to the questions posed by our scientific cultural river, we contend that the biblical text cannot be mined for scientific details or revelation. We cannot derive the physical scope or range of the event from the literary-theological presentation chosen by the biblical author. If asked, Was the flood global? our answer would be, Yes, it is global in its impact and significance, yet we have no reason to think that its physical scope and range was global. Since the Bible uses the rhetoric of hyperbole to describe the flood, it does not claim that the flood was universal in its physical scope and range; it rather portrays it in universalistic terms for rhetorical effect. If we turn to science, we find no evidence that suggests a global deluge. If science does not suggest a universal event, and the Bible (in our nuanced interpretation) does not claim a universal event, we have no reason to conclude that it was a universal event. Such a conclusion would diminish neither the authority of the text nor the significance of the event as unfolded in the interpretation of the author of Genesis.

Finally, what are we to think about a God who would do this? First, we should note that the Bible neither engages in theodicy nor invites us to do so. We are in no position to evaluate the justice of God. We are accountable to him, not he to us. God loves mercy and is compassionate, but a God who never executes justice would be no God at all.

Second, we must recall that the biblical text gives us only a limited knowledge of the inner workings of the divine mind. His ways are not our ways, neither are his thoughts ours (Is 55:8). We cannot know him fully; we can know only what he has revealed of himself. He has given us sufficient revelation so we might have some sense of his plans and purposes and trust him sufficiently to become participants in those plans and purposes. The flood succeeds in giving us insights into those matters. Our response ought to be to acknowledge the wisdom and authority of God. The fear of the Lord is the beginning of wisdom. We fear him by submitting humbly to his authority as the center of order wisdom.[2] We cannot understand all the factors that motivate what he does or the timing he chooses. We are not in a position to counsel him (Is 40:13-14; Rom 11:34); our response is to trust him.

---

[2]Wording suggested by John's student Rhett Austin.

For Further Reading

Bailey, Lloyd R. *Noah: The Person and the Story in History and Tradition.* Columbia: University of South Carolina Press, 1989.

Chen, Yi Samuel. *The Primeval Flood Catastrophe.* Oxford: Oxford University Press, 2013.

Copan, Paul, Tremper Longman III, Christopher Reese, and Michael Strauss, eds. *The Dictionary of Christianity and Science.* Grand Rapids: Zondervan, 2017.

George, Andrew. *The Babylonian Gilgamesh Epic.* Oxford: Oxford University Press, 2003.

Hill, Carol, Gregg Davidson, Tim Helble, and Wayne Ranney, eds. *The Grand Canyon, Monument to an Ancient Earth: Can Noah's Flood Explain the Grand Canyon?* Grand Rapids: Kregel Publications, 2016.

Horowitz, Wayne. *Mesopotamian Cosmic Geography.* Winona Lake, IN: Eisenbrauns, 1998.

Lambert, W. G., and Alan R. Millard. *Atra-Hasis: The Babylonian Story of the Flood.* Oxford: Clarendon Press, 1969.

Longman, Tremper, III. *Genesis.* Story of God Bible Commentary Series. Grand Rapids: Zondervan, 2016.

Lyon, Jeremy D. *Qumran Interpretation of the Genesis Flood.* Eugene, OR: Pickwick, 2015.

Ryan, William, and Walter Pitman. *Noah's Flood: The New Scientific Discoveries About the Event That Changed History.* New York: Simon and Schuster, 1998.

Walton, John H. *Genesis.* NIVAC. Grand Rapids: Zondervan, 2001.

————. *The Lost World of Genesis One.* Downers Grove, IL: InterVarsity Press, 2009.

Young, Davis A., and Ralph F. Stearley. *The Bible, Rocks and Time: Geological Evidence for the Age of the Earth.* Downers Grove, IL: InterVarsity Press, 2008.

Author Index

Subject Index

Scripture Index

Also Available

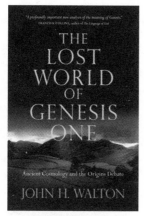

**The Lost World of
Genesis One**
978-0-8308-3704-5

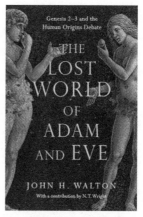

**The Lost World of
Adam and Eve**
978-0-8308-2461-8

**The Lost World of
the Israelite Conquest**
978-0-8308-5184-3

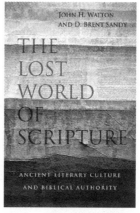

The Lost World of Scripture
978-0-8308-4032-8

Finding the Textbook You Need

The IVP Academic Textbook Selector
is an online tool for instantly finding the IVP books
suitable for over 250 courses across 24 disciplines.

ivpacademic.com